FOR RICHER, FOR POORER

FOR RICHER, FOR POORER

A KIND OF AUTOBIOGRAPHY

Johnny Speight

BBC BOOKS

Published by BBC Books,
a division of BBC Enterprises Limited,
Woodlands, 80 Wood Lane, London W12 OTT

First published 1973 by M & J Hobbs
in association with Michael Joseph Ltd
This edition first published 1991

ISBN 0 563 36269 3
Photoset in Baskerville by Redwood Press Limited, Melksham
Printed and bound in Great Britain by Redwood Press Limited, Melksham
Jacket printed by Clays Ltd, St Ives plc

Picture Credits
British Film Institute, Courtesy Viacom 6 (top);
Camera Press 4 (bottom);
Hulton-Deutsch Collection 1, 2 (bottom) 3, 5 (bottom);
Rex Features 6 (bottom);
David Secombe 8;
Courtesy of Johnny Speight 2 (top).
All other pictures © BBC.

CONTENTS

This book is dedicated to

Johanna Speight

née O'Sullivan

and

Constance Beatrice Speight

née Barrett

the two women of this

Parish – England

who have had the most influence

on my life

one my mother

the other my wife

who both contributed to my upkeep

at one time

or

another

1 Two up, two down and outside toilet

Two up, two down and an outside toilet. Bottom half to let. We had found a home. All we had to find now was the rent. The rent was 2s. 8d. per week which seems very little today, and only goes to show that they're charging much more now for the same old rubbish. I am sure that when my parents moved into what was to be their home for a decade, they were truly grateful. All they had to share was the front door and the toilet and so long as the people living above them were reasonably decent, things wouldn't be too bad. They were the same colour. That was a good start. Both families were Roman Catholic, so once the front door was closed on the world outside we had religious tolerance too. Naturally we had our disagreements. One was about where upstairs started and downstairs ended. The people upstairs insisted that the passage which led from the front door to the stairs belonged to us, and that it was our business to keep it clean. To which my father pointed out, if this were so, then they couldn't come in that way anymore.

The toilet raised a few problems. Obviously, it was less bother if you could manage to use it during the off peak periods only, and avoid it entirely in bad weather. The girl upstairs wouldn't sit out there on her own when it was dark, and her father had to accompany her with a flash light. He did this until she was married. We would hear her call out, 'You still there, dad?' And his shivering reply, 'Ain't you done yet?' Or, 'What you doing in there?' And, 'Won't be long.' With the bad plumbing you only had to smell it to realise why they built it outside.

We couldn't complain to the landlord because no one knew who he was. An old chap on a bike used to call and collect the rent. But first he had to catch us in. People used to knock on the door and say, 'The rent man's coming.' There was only so much money in the house and the art of collecting was to try and catch you with some of it left. We wore our best clothes on Sunday only. The rest of the week we worked to get them out of pawn. Some could afford to wear their best suit on a Saturday as well. Others didn't even have a best suit. There was one family where the men folk never wore shirts. Just a flat cap and scarf and trousers held up by braces. No one knew how they lived. All we knew was that nobody would live above them. By living the way they did they got the whole house to themselves. One of them did a bit of begging. But as far as I could see he was the only one that worked. His sister would show you her thing for two cigarette cards. I gave her two milk-bottle tops one day. But when I saw what it was I asked for them back.

Us kids would collect anything in those days. Used tram tickets, cherry stones. We kept the streets clean. We used to collect horse dung off the streets. It was free and it was good for gardens. When we did get a garden the only thing that would grow in it was a telegraph pole. There was only one telephone in the street and that belonged to the corner shop. They would let a few favoured customers receive messages on it. They once had a call from someone in Australia and all the street stood outside to watch them take it. Excitement ran high – and everyone asking if they could have a listen – and with the word spreading, 'They're talking to Australia round the corner,' more people arriving. More people – like people selling ice cream, soft drinks, hot dogs, balloons on a stick; there were even gypsies selling clothes pegs and fortunes.

This was before radio. Radio *had* been invented but the news of it hadn't reached Canning Town yet. We had to amuse ourselves still. The first radio set I ever saw had earphones. I was aware of an old fellow sitting there with things over his ears. And I thought he had something wrong with his ears. It was a kind of head truss he was wearing. And I heard someone say, 'Wireless! He's got wireless!' And I thought, 'Christ! That looks painful.' The doctors were discovering a lot of new diseases about that time. Well, new to us. Or perhaps they were just naming them. T. B. was the big one at the time. It all started with a concert pianist. He caught it playing the piano. And, of course, it soon spread to us. And people were dropping like flies with it. Very soon they were putting the cause down to certain kinds of work – such as coal mining, industrial labour and playing the piano.

Among the new diseases though was the new wireless set. Complete with battery and instructions. We stood our wireless set on top of the gramophone. This was a large piece of furniture with cupboard space for records. But as we had no records we filled the cupboard space with other kinds of rubbish. And when you got a big band like Ambrose 'playing on our wireless' the contents of the cupboards rattled. For years I couldn't stand Ambrose. I thought his band rattled. If you ever hear a big band with piano, bass and drums, full brass and sax sections and two cupboards full of odd bits of crockery and knives and forks you'll know what I mean. I used to think if Ambrose only got rid of the knives and forks his band wouldn't be too bad. And at other times I thought it was only the crockery that got in the way.

I can't remember when we got our first radio. We shared with upstairs for a while. Well, they had their radio up so loud there was no point in buying one of our own. In fact, people used to knock on the front door and ask upstairs if they could turn their radio even louder because there were people four or five doors along who couldn't hear it properly.

For a while the people who lived above us controlled the radio listening of twelve families. If they went out we asked them to leave their radio on. There was one big snag about this arrangement. The people upstairs went to bed early and no amount of persuasion could get them to leave their radio on for us. Anyway, their nerves were getting frayed with the arguments about what they should have on so we decided to buy our own. What further convinced us was that by now radios were beginning to fall off the backs of lorries and were getting cheaper. So through the friend of a friend who knew a feller we finally got our own first radio. Our popularity shot up and very soon people who normally only came in to borrow a cup of sugar started to 'stay the evening.'

At one time there were plans to pull our old house down and build a slum. But they haven't. I was back a little while ago looking for film locations for the first film of *Till Death Us Do Part* and I knocked on the door and it was opened by a black woman, one of five families that were living there then. Which is very interesting when you hear people say the world is shrinking and there isn't enough space for people. These people had found space where we couldn't. It really shows ingenuity. There was a house that seemed overcrowded to us. There's a lot to be said for enterprise.

When I was about twelve we moved – only four streets away – but it was a big move for us. It was almost a social upheaval. Some of the people in this new street even had aspidistras in the window. They all wore shirts. At the very top end they even wore collars and ties. The houses had bay windows. We still had an outside toilet. But now we had two rooms and a scullery downstairs and three rooms upstairs. I suppose a lot of people wouldn't have called the third room a room, but ... it slept two of us, for Christ's sake. We had a garden – a patch of black earth at the back of the house – and about two feet at the front. It gave us a feeling of substance. We could actually walk two feet away from our own front door without stepping on to the highway. We could actually stand on our own property. Well, our own rented property. The back garden was my father's joy. If a weed grew there, he'd rush out and water it. There were a lot of people a cut above us in the street. But we were a cut above the others. So I suppose that was some kind of progress.

Soon I began to realise that we weren't so posh as we thought because things happened and we moved around and saw even bigger houses. We saw houses that had at least six feet between the front door and the public highway. And we wondered at such affluence. They were probably 'regular workers'. That was the big thing then. Regular work. If you had regular work your credit was good. I suppose it still is. No one likes to lend money to people who haven't got any. Having regular work meant you ate regular and paid your rent regular and could go out regular without having to dodge the milkman or the rent collector.

It was my mother's ambition to move to Wanstead. They had grass in Wanstead. Grass is very fussy you know. Grass won't grow in some places. It won't grow under your feet despite what some people say – I know, we tried it. And the only space we had to grow grass on was nearly always under our feet. Grass is selfish, like most kinds of life. It only wants to grow for itself. And you can't expect it to grow where people keep on treading on it. You can't expect it to. It won't grow where cows keep on eating it. It wants its own life and not to be the source of other people's.

But there was a lot of grass in Wanstead. People would pack on to trams and rattle across to Wanstead with bottles of lemonade and sandwiches, and sit on the grass and picnic and look at the trees and have a high old time. You could still see houses. It wasn't that kind of country, in fact there were more houses than trees. You could see people lying on the grass with it sticking out of their mouths, sucking and chewing it. And it always gave me a comforting feeling 'cos I thought at least we're better off than they are – we don't have to eat grass.

And there was Woolwich. That had a free ferry. We used to go on this ferry; it was a paddle steamer. It was fantastic. We used to get on this big boat and go to the other side and back all day long. The fantasies we lived on that. It was built to ferry people and vehicles from one side to the other on business. But some days they couldn't get on. It was full up with us. Picnicking. There would be all these people and lorries waiting on either side. And us on the ferry singing and dancing to an accordion. And they couldn't get us off. We were entitled to a blow on the river and that was that. And we would nag at the crew to stop going backwards and forwards across the river and put upstream a bit. But they weren't catering for us. They just wanted us off. And the only way to be sure of keeping us off was to charge money.

5

Our big playground though was Southend-on-Sea. Cockles and whelks and broken bottles and paper hats on the beach. Drunks reeling among the traffic. The local peasantry weren't too keen on us. But we had money to spend. Our money was scruffy though. Well, although there wasn't a lot of money to handle, the bit there was got handled quite a lot. The people at Westcliff which was at the other end of the beach wouldn't touch our money. They put up their prices to keep us out. I think our money contravened their hygiene laws. It *was* filthy though. You'd be hard put to imagine where it had been the state it got in. It's still pretty filthy though in some areas. You can't keep it about your person. It'd rot your pockets. No wonder the banks burn it when they get it back. I look at some of it today and think, Christ, who's had this? If they can get their money in this state, what state must their homes be in. Dirty buggers! They should put a health warning in banks: *Please wash your hands before leaving this bank.*

Southend was only thirty miles or so away from where we lived but it was like going to an outpost of the Empire for us. We knew the natives were hostile but there was always enough of us so we didn't really have to mix with them. Anyway, we'd all been on a Ragged Children's outing so we were fairly thick-skinned. We used to stay in a boarding house. And I can tell you that every joke about seaside landladies is true. To get our money, they had to provide us with somewhere to sleep for the night, and a breakfast before they kicked us out in the morning. And an evening meal when they let us back in at night. And this they did with deep resentment. When we arrived they always asked us if we had bugs as though we kept them as pets. It's amazing that. They all thought we kept bugs like some people keep horses. I can't imagine what they thought we did with them. My father had enough to do without messing around with bugs. He had no money to spend on bugs or any other livestock hobbies. Some people kept a dog or a cat. Well, they gave them house room and the animal took pot luck. There was a pet shop on the corner where we lived that sold mice. You know, there were most of the people in the street trying to get rid of them and there was this nut trying to sell them. There was one chap who lived near us who

6

had a wooden leg, fifteen children and eight dogs. As kids we were frightened to pass their house in case they thought we were food. His wife was a big fat woman. How she got so fat and kept herself so fat was pure conjecture. She took in washing but they wore it before you got it back. People were getting their washing back in a worse state than they sent it. They took their milk off any doorstep. I think they were gypsies whose horse had died. *They* even kept bugs. They were either just having sores, or getting over them, or they were in full bloom and covered with some horrible greasy ointment. This family never went to Southend, I don't think they were allowed out of our street.

At Southend we could escape all this for a fortnight and enjoy the splendours of the sea – our island heritage. Why everyone associated the East-ender with cockles and whelks though I'll never know. I'm sure that most of them only ate them at Southend. It was the food of the locale or so we thought. The staple diet of the Southenders. The landladies of the Thames Estuary. What I can remember most about Southend was the washing in cold water and all drying ourselves on one damp towel. And that awful sand that got in your hair, your mouth, your ears, your pockets. It got everywhere. In the butter, the jam . . . I've always hated sand ever since. In every seaside town most of the people walk about with half the beach in their hair or their pockets. There was a builder's yard in Canning Town where they'd brush it out of your pockets for a shilling a ton. Happy days in Southend where you could pick your way gingerly over broken glass to stand knee high in the muck of the Thames. Hardly anybody goes there anymore. I think we got it a bad name. They'll even change dirty fivers in Westcliff today.

I preferred hop-picking in Kent to Southend. The natives were just as hostile but there were less of them. They didn't bother us very much so long as we didn't steal too much off them. Not that they had much to steal except a few apples, and we only nicked the windfalls. And the only reason why they didn't like us taking them was because while we had those we wouldn't buy their good apples off them. We kept earwigs there. And bugs. We found them in the straw beds. It was quite common there to see two bugs and a couple of earwigs sharing a matchbox. They became a kind of currency among the kids like cigarette cards. One kid we knew used to eat them. I don't know if he still does. Only in season probably ... and with good wine. Well, people do eat the most ridiculous things. I know a chap who eats squirrels. He says they taste like rabbits. And cats can pass muster as rabbit too. Still, I suppose it's where you eat that governs what you eat. The way things are going cat meat could become vogue in the West End. We were the descendants of the original Thames Estuary Mud Dwellers and there's no knowing what they ate. The popular diet among us is at the moment cow, pig, sheep and most bird life where we can catch it. But eating habits change and anything could get popular, I suppose. I hope it never gets to be people again.

Southend had the longest pier in England: a huge amusement arcade that stretched out to sea. Acres of McGill postcards. They're collectors' items now. We used to send them to our friends with a message scrawled on the back. Fools. We didn't realise how valuable they were. We should have kept all our comics, too. They're valuable now. We used to wrap our lunch in them. We didn't appreciate anything. We should have kept all our old rubbish and stored it till now. Everything – old cocoa tins, sugar packets, old newspapers ... stuffed fish in glass cases. We threw it all away. You see, today's rubbish could be tomorrow's treasures.

We were the first hippies. We wore anything. Old army uniforms, old police uniforms, football shirts. Fellers wore their sisters' knickers, girls wore their brothers' pants and we sat out on the doorsteps playing mouth-organs and singing and talking into the night. Those of us who didn't have to work that is. The difference with our Hippie Community was that if you didn't work you didn't eat. It wasn't all play. We couldn't beg. There was nobody to beg from. We used to borrow off each other.

We were a kind of surplus labour force. None of us in those days had professions or trades. We did anything. We used to go round the factories looking for work – and some of the strange revolting smells that came out of them . . . you couldn't tell what they were up to . . . they could have been boiling down people. We had no immigrant problems. Most of the people were trying to get out of our community not into it.

2 Nine years' hard

It is quite often asked, did I start writing at school? What was school like? It was something to escape from. It certainly made us appreciate the life outside. It was like the nick, only we hadn't done anything. It was built like a prison. If it had been offered to the Prison Authorities they would have turned it down. It wouldn't have met the requirements of the Prison Act. It was all right for children but it would have raised howls of protest if they'd dared to put convicts in it. The playground was more like a prison yard – it had a high wall around it with broken glass embedded in the top of it. We would get to this big yard and the head screw would come out and blow a whistle and we'd all form into lines. Then they'd call the roll to make sure there were no escapees. They would then march us into our various classrooms and our own screw would take over. First of all there would be a few cursory prayers in praise of the Lord who had allowed us to experience this pleasure. It was the same at school meals; we had to thank the Lord for the swill they dished out. The school meals were given to us free of charge. They could never have sold them. Not even to us. But we'd have a go at eating anything so long as we weren't asked to pay for it.

The only thing different between prison and school as far as I could see it was that to get into prison you had to go before a magistrate or a judge and jury whereas with us the sentence was automatic. Nine years' hard labour. They decry dictators for putting people in prison without trial but we were shut up for most of the day without trial. There was no Court of Appeal either. You had to serve your time. We got no remission of sentence for good behaviour and there was no Parole Board to review our case either. We used to plan escapes, or try and acquire a disease, anything to get out of school. We used to think you were lucky if you got T. B. If someone got T. B. we'd all try and catch it off him. If one of the kids had it we'd get him to breathe all over us, or spit on our sandwiches. I never had any fear of T. B. because by the time I realised I didn't want it, it was curable anyway. We envied other kids who got a lot of time off school with illness. The idea of school holidays I thought very sadistic. They only gave you a taste for the outside and when you had to go back again it was worse. It unsettled us. They were just giving us a taste of what we were missing. But I suppose they had to give the screws a rest otherwise they'd have broken under the pressure. But, I suppose, the reason why even the most enlightened of us support these prisons for the young is because without them what are we going to do with the little perishers? You don't want them hanging around you all day. The little people have their own way of life and most of the time it doesn't fit in with ours.

I learnt a few things at school, one of the most helpful being the ability to look interested when one isn't. This enabled me to avoid quite a lot of bother with teachers who didn't give a jot whether you were interested or not so long as you looked it and kept bloody quiet.

We would copy from each other where we could. Well, knowledge is to be shared, isn't it? If the boy next to you had the answer, well, it was labour saved, put it down and pray he was right. If he wasn't, and you were bigger than he was, then clout him. A lot of really clever boys would sweat over a problem knowing that if they got it wrong they were in for a rough time from the rest of the class. This wasn't a bad thing. It sharpened their brains and made life easier for the rest of us.

It was all part of our survival kit I suppose. If you can't work the thing out for yourself take someone else's answer and pray to God he's right. They're all at it: politicians are the worst. Most of them have never had an idea of their own. They beg, borrow or steal. They prefer to deal in second-hand ideas anyway. The only things they appear to value at first-hand are their wives, their clothes and their cars. It seemed to me that the whole idea of school was to vaccinate the pupils with a little specially prepared culture in the fond hope that it would enable them to resist it for the rest of their lives. With me, I suppose the vaccination didn't take and I made my first contact with culture through the instrument of great writers and it acted like a drug on me. And I became hooked on it. Now if I don't get my regular fix I am a most miserable person. My craving for culture is probably one of the best habits I have acquired.

What is wrong about our so-called educational system is that the wrong people are in charge of it. It is administered by local authorities on the cheap. And the people they appoint to educate the imprisoned pupils are quite often the most unsuitable, but the wages they offer unfortunately don't attract the really qualified people. Most of the people who profess to teach are suffering badly from a marked lack of learning themselves. Those who can do are doing and haven't the time or the inclination to teach especially at the starvation wages offered by the local authorities, usually amateurs themselves. Their concept of education is to take the ideas of truly great thinkers and grind them down to a convenient size and then spoon them into the pupil like some awful medicine, or purging powder, all the while holding his nose to overpower resistance: or beat them into his head with a stick.

We weren't allowed to talk in school. It isn't natural for a child not to talk, but like all lags we learned to talk out of the side of our mouths. We invented our own sign language too: that mysterious laughter of children when only they know the joke, and the joke is you, stems from some child rubbing its left arm to denote that you are a twit. That's what the little darlings do, only in our day it was a different word. Some of the words that all the fuss is about today were household words to us. And neither shock nor horror did we feel. They were looked on as bad words though – if what you mean as bad is not good. But then why should we have good words? Nothing else we had was any good. We took our words where we found them – in the gutter. They were our words. It was us who put them into common use. I could swear pretty good in those days. I could weave the words into some pretty lurid patterns. I've gone off lately. I suppose it's lack of practice. To me the only obscenity is poverty.

How you nurture the interest of a captive animal I have no idea. But you won't do it with long and short division, that I know. The captive child will endeavour to learn most things parrot fashion to escape the attentions of its gaoler, but this won't pass as education. For those who cannot escape over the barbed wire fences will surely escape into their own imaginations and dwell only on those thoughts that give them pleasure. Learning should be made a pleasure. If you can only gain a child's interest it is a most attentive animal. A child's mind is like its body: it needs bags of exercise. It needs fields to run in and trees to climb in order to exercise its limbs and it needs interesting problems to surmount in order to exercise its mind. But it doesn't need a gaoler to use its mind like a ragbag to stuff all the old beliefs, religions or moralities of its father into. I know teachers try to please but they should try pleasing their little charges more and not their parents. And by please, I don't mean giving in to all their nauseating little habits. For children are a problem, and the biggest problem is how to keep them out of sight and earshot while you get about your daily bread; as I said earlier, you don't want the little sods hanging about you in the office, and your secretary has got more to do than help junior build bricks and fill the inkwells with your clients' receipts. Besides, if she has got any spare time she can pour out some drinks and come and sit on your knee, and you don't want junior rushing home and telling mum all that goes on in daddy's office, do you? So, obviously, some-one's got to take them off your hands, but ensure that you put them into the hands of someone capable; someone who won't have to lock them up all day and beat them with a big stick or torture them in some other way. (The way some people teach is a refined form of torture practised mostly by intellectuals reduced

to this level.) And for Christ's sake, pay him enough to make the
job attractive to him. And make sure he's a man who regards the
words of the great poets as a pleasure to read and not as some
savage punishment to inflict on the hapless children he is in
charge of.

Anyway, I don't want to harp on this subject which is obviously
of so little interest to most of us that we allow it to go on un-
changed. It has been dealt with more fully elsewhere but never
gets publicised by newspapers except to complain that it doesn't
work which is becoming more and more obvious even to the
dimmest of us. Anyway, newspapers are not concerned with the
new. They're more concerned with guarding the old than publi-
cising the new. They're more a part of what was, than what is or
will be. Most of our newspapers are rapidly becoming nothing
more than sheets of adverts containing a few news items. They
stand with the Church, fading to seed as the new takes root and
grows alongside them.

The Church. There's a pack of lies. Everyone who was holy left
it years ago. What a bargain basement the Church is. No matter
how deformed your ideas the Church will find a religion to fit
them. It has many branches. It's got more branches than Marks
& Spencers. It sells everything. Once, it was like Woolworths,
with nothing over sixpence, but like everybody else it had to put
its prices up.

The Christian religion was set up two thousand years ago by a
Jewish carpenter of doubtful birth. He was an agitator of con-
siderable power, and was probably the first shop steward. He was
a more relentless negotiator than the present day Trade Union
Movement has ever seen. His terms were hard; harder than most
of us are prepared to put up with. He was an evolutionary force
few of us were ready for. He was God given to the working classes
of his day. But they ran away and left him at the barricades on his
own. He was vain. He thought he was God, and that kind of thing
always gets on people's nerves. They like to appoint their own
gods. But once he was dead and out of the way, they got a few
writers in to rewrite his life and make him a god posthumously.
They're still rewriting his life where they can. Our belief in

Christianity is evident in our marked lack of interest in each other.

Anyway, we kept the Ten Commandments as best we could. Most of them were easy.

Thou shalt not steal.

There was nothing worth stealing for miles around. You'd get yourself involved in a lot of travelling expenses before you found anything worth stealing.

Thou shalt not covet thy neighbour's wife, nor his ox.

You'll notice how his wife was bracketed with his ox. Man's wife has replaced his ox in modern society. Modern man couldn't afford a wife and an ox, so he ate his ox and put his wife between the shafts. Anyway, they didn't covet their neighbour's wives. Sex wasn't so important in those days. The average man in our community wanted a helpmate more than a plaything. If they were going to achieve any kind of standards at all, they couldn't afford the consequences of too much sex. Of course, some of them populated like rabbits and they were forced to live like rabbits in bloody hutches. They were fools. Even animals have the intelligence not to breed in a confined space.

Do not covet thy neighbour's goods.

Covet thy neighbour's goods! You never saw a rag and bone man round our street unless he was daft. He would probably have better gear on his cart than we were wearing.

Remember the Sabbath day, to keep it holy.

We observed the Sabbath as a day of rest. Christ, we needed it. You needed more than Sunday to get over our week. We went to church. It was one of the most popular dream factories around in those days and rated second only to the cinema. Very few of us wanted to be priests, though most of us wanted to be film stars. We put on our best suits every Sunday; it was the only day you could wear anything decent apart from Saturday night. Saturday night is the loneliest night in the week, so goes the popular song. In actual fact, it was the onliest night in the week. The night we'd worked all week for. Our night. The night when we were able to do almost what we pleased.

When we got to this better house, the house that had the two rooms downstairs that no one had to sleep in we had what you would call a sitting-room and a parlour. The room we made the parlour was always in the front of the house so we called it the front room. It was the room where we put all our best belongings on show so that people who called to visit or merely peered in while passing could see our way of life at its best. Here was the place for the piano, the best furniture, everything we held dear. The front room was only used on Sundays and High days. We knew that the only way to conserve these things in their almost new state was not to use them too much. On Sundays, we opened up the front room and lit a fire to air it – it was always damp in there. There were very few days during the year when it didn't need a fire to take the chill off it. We'd light the fire in the morning and by lunchtime it was just about warm enough to sit in. It was like a mini-Christmas day Sunday was, dull and dreary by afternoon. The worst kind of Sunday was a wet one.

We had a piano in the front room, but none of us could play it. It was useful though for standing pictures of the family on, and it filled up a space that would otherwise have remained empty. There were cigarette burns on the yellowing keys and inside it smelled a bit of stale beer. Quite a lot of us had these pianos and you could always hear someone practising the scales somewhere along the street. Few got past the scale stage. We used to hear a song on the radio and those of us who could read music would rush out and buy the song copy and try and play it for ourselves. Most of us though couldn't even read our language properly leave alone music. Of course, there were some naturally musical people who could pick out the tunes by ear. This was by far the best way as it didn't involve you in any expense. These fortunates were very popular and were always getting invited out to parties and were the centre of attraction in any room where there was a piano. They could play almost anything. They had a natural ear for music. I knew one chap who could read music faster than the average person could read the *Daily Mirror*. But he had no ear at all: if a fly settled on his music he'd play it.

All us kids used to visit our relations on Sunday mornings. It wasn't to see them, it was to cadge a few pennies. We would sit and stare at them until they gave us the money and then as soon as we considered it seemly, we would leave. That was, I'd say, a few seconds after they had given us the money. It was a collection we made every Sunday morning. Come rain or shine. You had to have been to church first though, otherwise you weren't eligible for the money. The first question they would ask was, 'Have you been to church this morning?' So it became imperative not only to go to church, but to be seen there. In order to draw our attendance in church to everyone's notice, we'd come in late and make a lot of noise tripping over the benches and dropping prayer books until we were certain our presence had been noted. If a priest was inclined to be long-winded, we'd avoid his session if we could. I mean, a long sermon cut down on our collecting time because you couldn't go there while they were having lunch. It would probably put them off giving you any money. It was a kind of protection racket. If they gave you a penny, they were protected against your presence for another week, and the sooner they gave it to you the sooner they were rid of you. The really shrewd ones had our money ready on the doorstep. 'Here you are!' they'd say. 'Don't bother to come in.' This was the way we liked it: it saved us having to sit there for half an hour or so looking at them, and they didn't have to look at us, or have us dragging our dirty boots up their passage. It's a pity they couldn't have sent us the money in the post – that way we wouldn't have had to see each other at all. But I suppose that wouldn't have worked because they'd have thought, 'Why am I sending him this money? I never see him.' So we really had to make our presence felt and go there and sit and stare at them before they'd shell out.

The front room was also used for parties. There were birthday parties, engagement parties, funeral parties, there were parties for going away and for coming back. The guests were mainly relatives. It's funny that friends were seldom invited to our parties. It could be that family ties were stronger in those days. We seemed to live closer together in those days. In each other's pockets almost. But I think the real reason why we didn't invite our friends was because we didn't want them to meet our relations. Friends you can choose ... relations you can't. Yet no matter how much you disliked them they were always invited. Most of us kids though weren't really concerned with the politics of the family. We were there for the nobbins. When they got drunk, they gave us money. It was trying to keep the family together that caused most of the rows. We were very insular. I've seen weddings where the bride's relations at the reception party would sit on one side of the room, and the groom's relations on the other, with neither side willing to make the first overture to friendship. But the most unreconcilable relations would mellow after a few drinks. It might end with a punch-up after they'd got enough drink inside them, and remembered that they couldn't stand the sight of the fellow and came back to their original form and whacked him.

Funerals were another getting together of the clans. People seemed to enjoy funerals and turned out in their hundreds for them in those days, lining the streets. Well, they were good theatre for all those not too involved in the actual happening. They did them well. Four black horses with large black plumes on their heads to every coach, the coaches themselves glistening with polish and covered with flowers, and they didn't break into a trot until they were at least four streets away. Families prided themselves on giving the deceased a good send-off. The poor buggers may not have had much of a life, but they left it with a bit more fuss than they came into it. It always seemed a shame to me; here was the most important day in the life of the poor departed, all these people thronging the street, weeping, and paying their respects to him; the pomp and stately gravity of his procession; never, in all his life, had so much attention been paid to him before, and there he was dead and unable to appreciate it.

'Would've done him good to see this,' I heard a woman say through her sobs as the hearse passed by.

'Oh yes,' her friend said. 'He wouldn't have missed it for the world.' And when the cars supplanted the horses another woman watching the funeral of a neighbour was heard to say,

'Shame! First ride he's ever had in a car that is, he would've enjoyed it.' Old quarrels were patched up while you paid your respects to the deceased, and any money you owed to

his descendants. It wasn't a question of the eldest son's inherit-
ance or where the dowager should live, but more a squabble
about who should have what, depending of course on what there
was to have. There wasn't much advantage in being the eldest son
in a working-class family, except you didn't have to be a 'second-
hand Rose' like the younger members of the family, who had to
wait for you to grow out of your clothes before they were handed
down. Being the eldest did have its disadvantages – you had to
break the boots in. My boots were always bought several sizes too
large so I could grow into them. And the soles were covered in
blakeys (metal studs) so they would last longer. My younger
brother had to get his wear out of them too. When I turned a
corner running fast showers of sparks shot from my boots. They
were lethal weapons too and prevented a lot of bullying. A kick
from one of those could put a leg in plaster for months. I grew up
trying to fit my clothes instead of my clothes fitting me. By the
time my clothes were the right fit, they were either too old to wear
any more, or they had to be passed on. Fortunately, by the time I
was big enough to fit into my father's old clothes I could afford to
buy my own. It's a sad thing about the poor, they are laughed at
as well.

When you're born poor you learn a lot of tricks about survivial.
Like by the time wartime rationing arrived we were used to it,
because for years we'd been rationed by poverty. Now we were
rationed by cards, which was an improvement. All it meant was
that they had to keep our food in the shop until we could save up
enough to buy it. They couldn't sell it to anyone else because it
was ours. We could even do a deal if it was meat and we waited till
late Saturday night and they had no fridge to keep it in. We were
Catholics and Friday was a meatless day. But when you're poor
nearly every day is a meatless day. So Friday was no big deal for
us. Being poor helped us to practise our religion easier. When
things got too bad, us kids were sent to bed early so we wouldn't
know we'd missed a meal.

My first job was lacquering spring clips. What they were used
for I have no idea. All I knew was they had to be lacquered. I
thought, 'Jesus, is this what it's all about? Is this what I went to

20

school for? Is this what I spent nine years in that broken-down academy for?' They didn't tell me anything about this while I was there. None of the teachers mentioned anything about lacquering spring clips. 'Christ,' I thought, 'I needn't have gone to that school. I could have done this when I was in kindergarten.' I had an uneasy suspicion though, even then, that there were certain people who would have had me lacquering spring clips instead of going to kindergarten if they'd had their way. These same people would have also agreed that my going to school was a waste of time and would much rather have had me working a lot earlier.

3 My future as a spring-clip lacquerer is threatened

Soon I was to fight in a war to protect my future as a spring-clip lacquerer in England's green and pleasant land. Personally I had no objections to a German having the job, it was a liberty I was quite prepared to relinquish along with all the other exciting prospects that democratic England had to offer me. But I was given no choice, it was either an army uniform or a convict's, and I was only just out of one prison.

I left that job after a few weeks. I told them to get a monkey. For a handful of nuts he'd have done it just as well. I was looking for work for a human being. But I was to discover there wasn't a lot of that kind of work going. So I jettisoned thousands of years of evolution and went back to being a monkey ... And it was work, sleep, work, sleep ... It's funny though how I'd rush out of that factory to get back down the street where we lived. When the hooter went I'd grab my coat and run like mad for home and when I got there ... I'd think ... WHY? Nothing was going to happen. After a while I got into the rhythm of things and walked.

My big ambition in those days was to become a white-collar worker. The job didn't pay any more but I was a snob I suppose. My schooling though hadn't fitted me for this kind of work. I hadn't got a school certificate. They were very fussy in those days who they let stick the stamps on their letters. If you were a

white-collar worker you could knock off work and go out in the
evening without having to wash. Washing was always a problem.
Bathing was a bigger one. None of the houses had baths. I used to
go to the public baths once a month – you know . . . 'More hot in
No. 9.' When I got a bit affluent I used the railway station baths.
There you controlled your own water flow . . . and you could
really soak . . . When the water got cold you let in more hot. But
day to day you only washed the parts that showed . . . face and
hands. Underneath you were filthy. If you ever took a girl out and
you got lucky and got under her clothes at all you always washed
your hands when you got home, especially if you were going to
touch food or anything. Knowing how you were yourself you
touched them very gingerly anyway. You'd be dancing with a girl
and you'd think, 'I wonder if her knickers are as dirty as my
pants.' It was offputting I'll tell you. It didn't leave you with a lot
of scope for romance. When you think of all those shitty arses
cavorting about the local Palais, smelling of Yardley's Lavender
and the local jam factory. I tell you they wouldn't have dared
wear seethrough then. The great unwashed, they sweated mud! I
went out with a girl who worked in a soap factory. She wasn't so
good-looking but where we had dirt she probably had soap so you
didn't mind chancing your arm. There was a chance you'd end up
cleaner than when you started. The first time with her she was
sweating and there were suds . . . I thought she had something. I
thought, 'Christ! It's the Lock Hospital.' You know, the Lock
Hospitals – they catered for V. D. holders. They used to advertise
in all the public lavatories. You called and said to the doctor, 'I've
called in answer to your advertisement.' Not many caught V. D.
but it's a wonder we didn't all go down with foot and mouth.
Despite their advertising campaign in the public lavatories the
Lock Hospital doctors weren't too keen to see you. I mean there
you were bringing them business . . . they thought you a dirty
bastard. They took their frustrations out on us as though we were
to blame for their not being allowed near the more fashionable
carriers of the posher diseases. It limited their shop talk for a start.
I mean, you could hardly go on about V. D. and its symptoms
over cocktails in those days. Not that half of them didn't have it

anyway. The medical profession at that time was still suffering under the delusion that V. D. was caused by too much sex. I knew a feller who caught it the first time he had sex and that was with his wife. I had a scare once. This brothel got raided in Belgium. The place was suddenly full of Military Police and one of them pulled me off the bed and reported me as a brotheliser and V. D. suspect. The M. O. immediately placed the cookhouse out of bounds to me and made me wash my eating utensils separately from the other men and perform my ablutions in private. An old soldier said to me,

'You don't want to worry about it. You'll soon know if you've got it.'

'How?' I said.

'Your prick'll fall off,' he replied. His sex tastes were simple. He was happy with anything. He'd sup his sexual pleasures any- where. One night he told me how to fuck a goat. You put its hindlegs down the front of your wellington boots if you're interested. This is to stop it kicking out at you and running away. Which forces one to the conclusion that goats don't like being fucked by old soldiers.

When you bought a decent suit you also bought problems. The main problem was keeping it decent. I remember one suit in particular. It was a pale blue gabardine. A pretty daft colour to wear in Canning Town. That suit was never out of the cleaners'. When I wore that suit I would walk three miles to the station rather than take it on the bus. It was a working bus. It worked hard all day taking people to work in the mornings and bringing them home again at night. They didn't have time to clean the bus before people started going out again in the evening so they didn't bother. The first night I wore this suit I got on the bus without thinking. The floor of the bus was ankle deep in cigarette ends and other rubbish that had been dropped during the day and the grease shone through the dust and grime on the seats. I couldn't sit on any of the seats with this marvellous pale blue suit on so I spread the newspaper I was carrying on the seat and sat on that. I spread another piece of the newspaper over all the crap on the floor to keep it off my new shoes. They were white when I started the journey. I had just settled down when this feller got on and sat down beside me, his working clothes brushing against mine. I squirmed away as far from him as I could, which wasn't far, and every time the bus lurched he fell against me. It was awful, the fear I had of getting that suit dirty on the short trip on the bus to the station. I hated this feller sitting next to me. He seemed to be rubbing against me all the time. What made it worse he leaned across me trying to read the paper I had spread on the floor. Another thing I didn't realise till later was that I'd got newsprint on the seat of my trousers also. You weren't supposed to wear light colours in that sort of area. You wore clothes that didn't show the dirt. You also used wallpaper and paint that didn't show the dirt. The dirt was there but it didn't show. That's why we painted everything dark greens and browns. A house with light wallpaper or painted white was unheard of. Even the white-collar workers were very grubby white-collar workers.

War broke out, and I became aware that my existence was known to the Government. I should have sent their letter back ... not known at this address ... and that I had no experience of this kind of work anyway ... and besides war work wasn't what I was looking for ... But ... the Government was set on having this war with Hitler and they issued the challenge on behalf of all of us it seemed.

I joined up at Stratford. Not Shakespeare's Stratford, Stratford East which was a huge collection of slums, the homes we were being asked to defend with our lives. (Hitler's bombing of London was the biggest slum clearance operation the city has ever known.) It was a Signal Regiment I joined, but the only wireless set any of us had ever seen was the one on the sideboard at home. I remember thinking that if the rest of the army was like us we might as well surrender now. I had seen the German army on newsreels and they looked a lot more formidable than we did. Most of us were still going home for lunch and a lot more of us were still sleeping at home because they hadn't got enough accommodation for us. I got the feeling that Chamberlain must have declared war without telling the army anything about it. It seemed to me that they hadn't heard about it any earlier than we had. In fact, I got the distinct impression they had only heard about it on the radio or read about it in the newspapers the same way we had. My only consolation was that perhaps the Germans hadn't heard about it yet either. Most of us were still wearing civvies. None of us had seen a gun yet. In fact the only thing I'd seen that resembled a weapon in any way was the stick the Colonel carried under his arm and used for poking us with. Perhaps they were going to issue us with boxing gloves and kit us out with shorts and vests with Union Jacks on the front. It seemed that both Germany and England had chosen France again as the battleground. No wonder the French don't like us, we always pick their backyard to fight in. England v. Germany. Venue France.

I was on the wharves then. I was a plater's mate. A lot of workmen had mates in those days. There were carpenter's mates, electrician's mates, plumber's mates, you name it and he had a mate. I suppose they had to give them a mate otherwise they wouldn't do the job. It was someone to talk to. Someone to make their tea for them and carry their tools. You had to be a bit shrewd otherwise you'd find yourself doing most of the work while he sat and talked to you. This plater would tell me all his troubles about how his wife wasn't giving him enough or about how many times he had it each night and how good all these women said he was and how big their tits were and how he would stick it between them and shove his head between their legs; how he shoved it up their arse, in their mouth, in their ears and in the middle of all this he'd take it out and stir his tea with it, or he'd put it between a couple of slices of bread and make out it was a sandwich. His humour was quite basic. If he could have driven rivets in with it he'd have been a much happier worker. They should have called him up the day war broke out and stuck a bayonet on the end of it. Another product of our educational system, he had this great thing between his legs and nothing between his ears. He was just a big prick. He had all this equipment that needed regular exercise – it kept him awake all night. While other fellers were relaxing he was out drumming up work for it – sales chatting girls to keep it fully employed. It seemed to have a life of its own. Whenever it was hard he had it out showing it off, measuring it and waving it about. It's wonder he didn't paint it West Ham's colours and wave it from the chicken run at Boleyn. It looked like a bloody great cobra and he talked about it as though it had a mind of its own. If a girl walked past it would raise its bloody great head and he'd pat it and say, 'He knows. Look at him. Look. He'd be up there. Down boy.' And he'd tuck it back into the top of his sock with a wistful look. I don't know what his wife thought about it. He reckoned he used to poke it into her like a ferret into a rabbit hole and it would poke its ugly head out of her mouth and wink at him. I would feel embarrassed bringing mine out in the gents alongside of his. I mean, Christ, mine was a different species.

Once we had put on the King's uniform and taken his shilling we were obliged to live by a different set of rules to the ones we had been brought up with. For instance, thou shalt not kill didn't apply anymore. That commandment had been suspended, and hardly out of one school we were now into another with butchering high on the curriculum. Very soon now I was to encounter the stench of death. You see it on television now but they are freshly killed corpses posing in death for the cameras. What we were to see were sometimes a week old or more and nowhere near as tidy looking. Christ, that smell, the smell of rotting bloated corpses. It is a smell that is hard to recall and equally hard to describe. There are no words to describe it. The smell of what was once a battlefield is a sickening stench that I could actually taste and feel in my mouth and which, made me shudder violently and hold my breath. I was filled with the kind of terror that animals must feel when they approach the slaughter house. And then to watch others with stronger stomachs than myself actually looting these bloated remains. Grabbing the shoulder to turn the body over, putrefaction oozing as the trunk moves leaving the arms, legs and head still face down, and stirring the stench, and all for a few evil smelling marks or a cheap watch. I suppose it does no real harm to rob the dead. They have no need of money where they're going and less need of time.

I was one of a party detailed to cremate these dead by pouring petrol over them and setting fire to it. They didn't burn well. You had to keep raking at them and adding more petrol in much the same way you would burn a pile of wet leaves in the garden. I don't know why they swell to such a size but it didn't help. And then the rakes would keep getting caught in the rotting mess and I would keep being sick and a fucking fool of an officer shouting, 'Steady on with that petrol.' We couldn't bury them. There were too many and there was no bloody time. Anyway they were Germans and it was a hot summer, and none of us were keen for a lot of digging. And they didn't seem too fussy about their last resting place. They were quite content to lay there and rot. The flies buzzing noisily and the working maggots growing visibly fatter as you watched.

And another day equally hot and the great pit hastily dug in the clay of a field just outside of Caen being filled with the bodies, blood seeping through the covering blankets off-loaded from trucks and the priests of all denominations buzzing noisier than the flies at the grave edge. These were our boys and we would perform what last rites we could and cover them with earth away from the worried eyes of their companions at arms. They were a pithead division from Newcastle so they wouldn't mind so much the overcrowding of their last earthly resting place. They'd been overcrowded in life ... sharing their beds with their brothers and sisters ... and lived shoulder to shoulder at the coal face ... and died shoulder to shoulder facing the enemy. Some of them were being scraped from the trucks, their bodies incomplete ... their legs and arms scattered Christ knows where ... fields apart. Nature could still find work for them fertilizing the fields of France. And onward surged the Second Army leaving death and destruction in its wake.

Christ we didn't half make a mess of France, Belgium, Holland and Germany. I remember the Falaise Gap as they called it, it was like a huge volcano had erupted. There wasn't a brick left standing. We certainly liberated the people of Falaise. We certainly cut them loose from the burden of their possessions. I greeted one old man coming out of the ruins of his home.

'Bonjour,' I said in French.

'Piss off,' he said in English. I mean, we didn't expect them to garland us with flowers and throw champagne parties in our honour, but we thought they might have shown a little pleasure. I mean, after all, we were liberating them and it wasn't our fault the Germans were holed up in their homes. I suppose our way of liberating them was a bit like blowing up the house and burning it to the ground in order to get rid of burglars but there was no other way, or at least, no other safer way. Our artillery and aerial bombardment was terribly effective; it was so effective, in fact, that the only Germans I saw at that time were either dead or prisoners of war. It was hard on the French and their villages, but it made things a lot easier for us. Anyway, at that moment in time, the Allied High Command weren't bothering too much about how the French felt. I mean, after all, they were only civilians, and foreign ones at that; and the way this particular war was going civilians were rapidly having to take a back seat as far as consideration went.

Hitler started this trend with his blitzkrieg. Hitler, I suppose, brought a perverse kind of democracy into war in the sense that when he was dropping high explosive bombs he wasn't fussy who he dropped them on. Prior to Hitler, wars were fought out only by soldiers – and never in England. In all our wars up until then, unless you were a member of the Armed Forces, you saw very little action. The bombing of our major cities was our first taste of civilian warfare and we didn't like it. The German High Command were branded as criminals, and the reason for these high born and well brought up men sinking to such depths of degradation blamed on the evil influence of Hitler. The bombing of women and children was a disgrace the Germans would never live down. The fact that the average British soldier was no more than a child and that most women were busily engaged on war work was not taken into account: nor the fact that in all of our industrial towns everyone, women and children included, lived next door to the factories where, with the best intentions, the bombs were directed. Neither did it stop us doing the same thing in France and Germany once we had the tools to do the job. And do it we did with no compunction or regard for human life.

There was a good chance of getting a leg blown off here, or an arm or two, and let's face it, there wasn't exactly a glittering career waiting in civvy street even for the able-bodied; and as I couldn't see band-leaders falling over each other to sign up a limbless jazz drummer, and as I didn't want to trade my drums for a tray of matches, I decided to stay as clear of trouble as I could without being actually shot for cowardice.

So far, I hadn't been doing too badly. Apart from the bombing in England, this was my first action. I had also missed the worst part of the invasion and had managed to stay in England until D Day plus about 60 – well, when I arrived in France they were sunbathing on the beaches. I was also an Artillery cook and although you had to take a lot of shit from your own side as well as the enemy it was better than being in the Infantry. And so I thought, if I can survive through this big offensive into Germany there's a reasonable chance of my getting out of this lot intact. Which I did. The nearest I came to serious injury was when we were dive-bombed and machine-gunned by American aircraft. I remember a lance-corporal shouting out to us as we dived for cover, 'It's all right! They're ours!' They were the very last words the poor bastard spoke. I don't know what fool had mistaken us for Germans. We were medium artillery and well behind the front line infantry – or should have been. But there you are, the people who run wars are the same people who run governments and you only have to listen to those in opposition to realise how stupidly incapable most of them can be.

I remember seeing a Lysander observation plane shot down out of stupid bravado. They were known as flying jeeps and we used them as eye for the guns. They would hover over enemy positions and direct our fire. This one was attacked by two enemy fighters. The O. I. C. reported the oncoming action,

'I think we're on to something. Jerry's annoyed. He's sent up a couple of Stukas.' If Jerry was that annoyed the berk should have got the hell out of there right away – no messing. He was a sitting duck for planes like that. But he didn't and we lost an expensive aircraft, a bloody good, if foolhardy, officer and a highly trained signalman, and all at no cost to the Germans at all.

Planes used to fly low over our position on their way back to England from raids over Germany the crew waving to us thumbs-up style, and us drinking tea out of mess-tins that still contained the stains of baked beans and tinned sausages and the grease from the washing-up water.

Standing on top of a hill watching a thousand-bomber raid with H. M. S. *Rodney* firing over our heads, and feeling good as the flames lit the sky and the continuous thud of high explosive that seemed to go on all night softening up the enemy. The ground reverberating under our feet as our own guns joined in the action and those thousands of spiteful-sounding twenty-five pounders that almost drove us mad with their incessant snapping. (The Germans thought they were our secret weapon and prisoners asked us about these terribly efficient little guns – they thought they were belt-fed like machine guns.) And in the morning, still finding that after all this colossal bombardment the bastards still had to be winkled out of where they were dug in.

And the bastards returning our fire. I hated being shelled. It was worse than being bombed. Bombing by aircraft was still pretty much indiscriminate but when we were being shelled we knew it was us the bastards were after. They would send a few range finders and then, when they were on target, all hell would break loose and the Germans were, if nothing else, shit hot when it came to aiming their big guns. They could drop a shell like Johnny Haynes could drop a football on a sixpence. And I was bigger than a sixpence and worried shit scared.

I thought then, and I haven't changed my opinions much since, that when old men start wars then those same old men should be made to go and fight them. It would save the lives of a lot of youngsters and get rid of a lot of decrepit senile old fools. When these bloody fools start wars they're at the end of their own time anyway and if they're so bloody stupid that they can't run the world without behaving like murderers every twenty years or so, they are better off with their Maker, always providing they are the kind of company He wants to keep. Personally, I think the man with the big fork is far better company for them.

And then the war with Germany finished and I got sent with thousands of others to a holding battalion somewhere in France. It was a place they broke up units and refitted them and sent them out to the other war that was going on in Japan. Our Japanese or Far Eastern Branch as it were. When they dropped the atom bomb and rang the curtain on that war too, I heaved a big sigh of relief I don't mind admitting. The full horror of it didn't penetrate at that time and if it had I don't believe I would have felt any differently. It was away with the guns and back to my drums for me and not a day too soon.

The first thing I cottoned on to in this holding battalion was not to answer my name when it was called out. My face was unknown here. I had had my anonymity restored to me and when the name of Signalman Speight was called over the tannoy I just cocked deaf-uns, and spent some of the most marvellous months of the war there, just lying pleasuring myself in the hot sun, listening to Frank Sinatra and all the bands of the A. F. N. My days consisted of joining the breakfast queue and then shirt off in the sun until the N. A. A. F. I. queue was formed and then back to the sunny grass until the dinner queue, and so on all through those lazy hot days.

But all good things come to an end, and the camp was getting dangerously empty and so I and the rest of the ragbag lot that were left finally did what all good soldiers should do and answered to our names and numbers smartly before it became chargeville. And so with the rest of the remnants I was sent back to England and into another kind of holding battalion for Japan and Burma. I became the R. S. M.'s batman almost as soon as I arrived there, which was a very good number because he was the man who picked the ones who were due for the big trot across the water to far away places, and he wasn't going to pick me because I was rapidly becoming indispensable to his comfort. His Sam Browne and boots shone the Colonel's and all the other officers' to shame. I was an experienced cook and rowed myself in among the hierarchy of the camp cuisine. My Sergeant Major was eating as well, if not better than anyone during those lean years of rationing. If four eggs, a half pound of bacon and all the fried bread and beans he could stuff down his ugly gullet was his idea of a good breakfast, he was getting it . . . and more. I was so well in that once when a new sergeant got a bit nasty with me, like putting me on guard duty, I informed the Sergeant Major while he was drooling over his gargantuan breakfast that this new feller was making things a bit difficult and that because of him I hadn't been able to prepare his breakfast as I would have liked to and the following week our new three-striped friend was being seasick somewhere on some ocean on his way to fight the Japs.

So that was the Army. Or some of it. I wasn't concerned too much about who won the war so long as I survived it. I really couldn't see how German masters could be any worse or any more ill-natured than my present British masters were. If the Germans had come to Canning Town, I don't suppose they would have stayed long. They might have made us slave labour, but I was that anyway. And what I have seen of Germans since the war they compare favourably with most Englishmen I know. I consider myself a world citizen with leanings, very strong leanings, towards England – the best of England, that is.

After they dropped the BOMB I went to Catterick to await demob. Catterick was a bit horrifying actually because the army mentality was taking over there with a vengeance and they were getting back to all the old bullshit again. Like whitewashing coal and all that crap. They put us in some brand new barracks all centrally-heated with showers and every mod con. I got out of there as fast as I could and into a little primitive slum stoking the boilers that fed the central heating and supplied the hot water for the showers, et al. A Nissen hut that no one bothered with on inspection days. It was hidden away in a kind of derelict no-man's land. All the visiting VIPs ever saw was the big modern block and the bullshit in there was terrifying. They were cracking under the strain with the blanco jitters and the polish bends. They had to sleep at attention the poor bastards.

Where we were was a kind of stokers, cooks and quartermasters staff complex. The untouchables. And we were allowed to wallow in our own shit. We were near enough semi-demobbed, and augmenting the civilian staff of N. A. A. F. I. and other odd bods. I found it very much to my taste at that time and when I finally got demobbed and chucked out of the Army back into civvy street and had to start working in factories again, it came as a bit of a shock. And often walking down to the Labour Exchange I really regretted leaving Catterick. It was marvellous. All the bods in our little complex were to my taste. They were fellow layabouts. Shirkers rather than workers. They didn't believe in work or anything like that at all. All they believed in was getting ponced up and parading their attractions around the local dance halls. And attractions we had plenty of – like butter, tea, sugar, bacon, chocolates and all kinds of rationed goods to give a girl who wasn't too hung-up morally. Our billet was full of birds. Birds for Butter was our slogan. A pound of sugar was a good leg-opener in Catterick in those days.

We could all fiddle new uniforms and when we weren't fulfilling our duties, stoking the fires or cooking the meals or dishing out rations, we were lying on our beds pressing them. We did look smart when we went out in the evenings. In our complex we had all the layabouts that were in charge of rations and all the other little necessities of life. It was where the real power lay in a lot of ways. I suppose we were a kind of small-time Mafia. Extra food was brought in by the chaps who worked the cookhouse and we had fry-ups at anytime and all times of the day and night.

In this slum block was every comfort the modern block never had. There was continual piping hot water in the showers. That was a first priority, that and the officers' quarters. Any complaints from there and they would be down looking for us and we weren't the sort of people who wanted bother of that kind. The officers' quarters were kept in perfect condition. Their heating etc., was spot on and their food lavish. The only block that suffered was the modern block. They sometimes had no hot water in their modern showers and baths, but by the time they complained and an orderly officer had time to get there, the water was hot again and they'd get told off for complaining and dragging an officer out into the cold to investigate. So they didn't complain much.

It was marvellous when we went out socialising, we would put on all our best clothes, all the gear, and we looked really smart. We didn't have to wear our best clobber for parades and all that rubbish like they had to in the modern block. They were in their best uniforms drilling all day, the poor bastards. It was heart-breaking for them trying to keep their uniforms up to scratch for parades and all that bullshit without the added effort of keeping them in good nick for pleasure as well. Anyway, they were so tired, they hadn't got the energy to go out at night on the town. They couldn't raise enough steam for a wank after one of their days. But with us, we'd have a lazy day fucking about in the boiler room in dirty old overalls and when we were finished we got showered and prettied ourselves up, had a good meal from the illicit food cooked in the boiler room – a meal of bacon, or steak and eggs, chips, fried bread, the lot, swilled down with mugs of hot sweet tea. Not very good for our figures, but very good for our morale and sense of well-being. Then we'd be off out, like play-boys of the western world.

Also, little things like money didn't bother us as we had the wherewithal for everything. If we wanted to travel further afield on our nocturnal pleasures, there was always the quarter-master's transport and bags of petrol to run it with. Oh yes, it was a darling time we were having, the horrors of the war fading rapidly into the distance, and the new horizons of civvy street looming nearer every day and the glittering career of a jazz drummer just waiting to be taken up – or so I thought then.

4 Butter – nine months a pound

I got caught once taking home rations. I got picked up by two of the Military Police just as I was about to cross the Thames by way of the Woolwich Ferry, one of my earlier happy childhood playgrounds. I was a fool really. We were stationed in Kent at the time, and I was on a week-end pass taking home some sugar, tea and butter etc. I was an idiot to go through Woolwich though. It was a big barrack town, a huge parade centre, and bullshit mad. I was with this working battalion and we were nowhere near as smartly turned out as those square bashers in Woolwich. In addition I was particularly scruffy, looking more like a desert rat than a soldier serving his time in England. Fashions catch on, and at that time most of us affected the style of the Eighth Army. Some of the officers took the wire out of their caps and tried hard to look like Rommel even to standing up in their jeeps as they rode through the Kent lanes. As I walked through the streets of Woolwich I stood out like a sore thumb, with the neck of my tunic undone and a scarf tied round my throat, my knapsack hanging over my shoulder, the brass on it dull to green almost as I slouched along, more like a tramp than a soldier. I suddenly saw these two M.P.s and shot into a doorway, but they had seen me and made towards me. I saw the ferry about to pull out and wondered whether to make a dash for it, but these two M.P.s looked a bit big and pretty athletic, and I thought they might turn nasty and whack me if I made them run. They were evil-looking sods and they could have done this and got away with it, my being an escaping prisoner like. Already in their minds I was a prisoner. I was their catch for the day. I mean, they had so many charges, 'improperly dressed', 'not properly dressed', 'scruffily dressed', plus the booty which now hung heavily from my shoulder.

'What you got in there?' they said.

'Dirty washing,' I said.

'Let's see it,' they said, and pulled it out.

'Where d'you get this from?'

'From my mother. I'm taking it back. I borrowed it for manoeuvres.'

Then of course they put the local Sherlock Holmes on the case and he found rice in the tea, and they knew that the only place you find rice in the tea was in an Army cookhouse. Then they got real nice and friendly and said that they didn't want to run me in as I looked honest enough, and that as I was a nice clean decent respectable looking lad would I do the sensible thing and grass on the others. I said, 'What others?' And they said that they knew I wasn't the only one at it, and that there were others worse than me, and that they didn't want me to take the can for these other bastards who had been fly enough not to get caught yet, and a lot of other crap in the same vein. 'No,' I said. For one thing I didn't trust the evil sods. I didn't tell them this because they were nasty bastards and it wouldn't have been shrewd to get cheeky with them. I could really have given them a list of names though, from the colonel downwards . . . The quartermaster was shitting bricks from the time I was arrested – and so he should. He needed more than a knapsack for what he was taking home to his mother. He had a lorry three or four times a week. I had the feeling he was supplying either the British Home Stores or another army. But I didn't grass. Well, there was no point, we were all living together and were going to be living together for a long time yet . . . the war was dragging on and it wouldn't have done me any good to grass on the others.

I was finally sentenced to nine months in Sowerby Bridge

detention barracks and did about five. My colonel got me released in the end by appealing to the War Office on the grounds that the Regiment couldn't pull its full weight in the war with a highly skilled member of it doing time. At least, that's what I like to think. Anyway, he got my prison or nick time commuted.

I got on all right in there, again because I used my wits and found out what the score was and teamed up with the local snout baron – the source for smuggled cigarettes. Snout was the currency in the nick and you could swap it for extra diets and it also enabled the snout baron and I to employ a batman. I saw fellows in there smoke their bootlaces and drink metal polish. How the snout got in there was through the screws, the gentlemen who ran the establishment, and the money to buy it off them came in through visits to the prisoners. Also I found two other sources of supply which helped to keep our stock high and fresh. I got a job in the library which kept me off square bashing. The librarian was in the Army Educational Service, and was a pimply faced lemon with great big glasses, a stoop, and shitty coloured skin. He stank with halitosis and this is probably why I thought his skin looked shitty, it was I suppose an association of ideas. I think it gave him a feeling of security that he'd found someone who liked books, or rather professed to like books. I wasn't keen on books in those days but the job was a good one and I'd profess to liking almost anything then for the sake of an easier life. The screws never used the library, nor did the prisoners. The kind of literature they wanted was more in the pornographic line.

The librarian was a liberal-minded man and he always left me twenty fags to nick. He hated the whole idea of the prison system but he was too scared to leave it in case they gave him a gun and put him in the real army. So he'd found a little niche in the safety of Sowerby Bridge and these packets of cigarettes kind of salved his conscience. He was no fool. He was busy surviving as well. Fear makes cowards of us all.

I also had a part time job helping the dentist and he left cigarettes out as well. Unlike the librarian he never left full packets and again, unlike the librarian, he never told me I could have them, so I had a suspicion that I might be nicking them. But

I didn't let it worry me too much and he never complained about missing them. For an army dentist he wasn't bad actually. If you had a tooth that needed pulling out he could get pretty close to it.

I saw fellows in there reporting for Holy Communion. It was the bread and wine they'd heard about that was the attraction. They thought they were going to get another breakfast.

The night screw had his hands full trying to keep us quiet after lights out. They kept us in cages. Twenty or so to a cage and four cages to a floor. A voice would shout,

'Screw. I want to go to the pictures.'

'Look in the mirror. You're a pretty picture yourself.'

'But I want to see the moving pictures.'

'I'll make you move if I put these lights up!'

Or,

'I'm frightened of the dark, Screw.'

'Shurrup!'

'Mummy always gives me a nightlight.'

'Shurrup!'

We had a latrine bucket in the cage and one of us was responsible each day for emptying and cleaning it. It had to be bloody polished too. And if it was a big fellow on bucket duty you were frightened to shit in it in case he thumped you. It was awful. But if you were a little fellow and puny . . . Christ you got a bucket of shit to slop about emptying next day. They saved it up for you, the bastards.

They put bromide in our cocoa to stop us getting randy but I don't think it worked well because there were an awful lot of stiff blankets each morning I believe, and there was a married couple in our cage. We heard them grunting away at it one night and the fellow in the next bed to me said,

'Which one puts it up whose arse I wonder?'

I was never sure if they were real queers or just trying to work their ticket. Some of them got up to all sorts of tricks in order to work their ticket. Well over sixty per cent of the inmates of a military detention barracks are military delinquents of some sort. A lot of them were people who had been on the run since the war started and as soon as they were released they'd be off again.

There was one fellow there who would only wear his uniform back to front. They gave him bread and water, solitary confinement and then he began to walk sideways. Before I left he'd taken to drilling himself backwards up and down the cage all night. There was another fellow who, during all the time I was in this Army nick, wore nothing but a blanket and kept cutting himself at every opportunity. He wasn't allowed eating irons or anything sharp. Not even a mirror. I don't think the lack of a mirror bothered him too much – he was an ugly bastard. If I had a face like his I wouldn't want to look at it too often. I don't know how he shaved himself. Here was a fellow who wasn't much use to the Army but still they kept him. These two were always being visited by various Army psychiatrists. One day they brought an ex-Harley Street head-shrinker in to see one of them. He was kitted out as a General, and this nut threw off his blanket and started to wank in front of him. One of the fellows on broom duty who saw it said it was hilarious. He told us that the General kept saying,

'Control yourself, my man. Control yourself.'

And the nut kept laughing and saying,

'Slip 'em off, baby. Come on. Don't be shy. Look what Daddy's got for you.'

And the screws piled in with the boot and everything trying to get the blanket back on him – and the nut was shouting,

'Go away you jealous bastards. Let me slip him a length.'

They finally got him quiet with a stool. Later he half killed a screw with the same stool. He was a wild man. They had to take his food in four-handed.

I had to go on the boxing team there to pick up snout that had been stashed in the gym. The P. T. instructor was a source of supply. I got a lot of teeth knocked loose there and a liberal dose of gingivitis which, with the lack of mouth hygiene prevalent in a Military Detention Barracks, broke into a gallop, bringing my teeth and gums almost to a parting of the ways.

I was up in the cage one morning giving a high polish to the shit bucket. This bucket was a typical example of military mentality, it had to shine until it hurts your eyes, yet the utensils we ate from left a lot to be desired. Our shit was served to the sewage farm in shining buckets while our food was served in near rusty cans. I don't know what one of their pet khaki clad psychiatrists would have made of that. Anyway, I was up in the cage distributing equal shares of metal polish and elbow grease to our shit receptacle, and there was a young lad there, just arrived, laying his kit out in the altar formation required. He had been given six months for running away to see his wife have a baby. He was a big softy the lad, and his crime didn't merit six months in this crap hole. He had placed a picture of his young wife atop the mound of equipment on his bed and this screw saw it, and went berserk.

'What you gonna do with that? Wank in front of it?' screamed the screw.

'No, sir.'

'You don't call me sir!'

'Sorry sir.'

'Sergeant!!!'

'Sergeant.'

'And when you call me sergeant make it sound like sir!'

'Yes, sergeant.'

'Sir!!!'

'Sir.'

'Three days bread and water for not obeying an order!'

'Yes, sir.'

'Sergeant!!!'

'Sergeant.'

'Sir!!!'

'Sir.'

'You're trying to make it hard for yourself ain't you?'

'No, sir.'

'Yes, sir!'

'Yes, sir.'

'Sergeant!!!'

'Yes, sir, sergeant.' And blubbered into tears.

The screw then took the picture of the lad's wife and tore it into shreds, while the lad sobbed. A big evil bastard of a man, Ginger Hawkins, who was on broom duty in the corridor, and had watched all this with me, grabbed the screw by the throat and half throttled him. He then hit him splitting his eye wide open. The screw went down and the boot went in, again and again until the screw was a grovelling heap spitting out teeth and all sorts, and Ginger's boot was a bloody mess.

'Now put me on report, screw, and I'll fucking swing for you,' he snarled. 'I will. I'll fucking swing for you.'

I was surprised. Really surprised. I would never have thought that Ginger Hawkins was a man capable of such sensitivity.

5 Howard Wynn-Jones & his big broadcast band

Before the war I played the drums in people's front rooms. There were two of us, a piano player and myself and we called ourselves The Syncopated Rhythm Boys. The piano player wasn't very good. His big idol was Charlie Kunz who was also pretty lousy in my opinion. Charlie Kunz's signature tune was *Here Comes Charlie* and this piano player wanted to make it ours and start off all our parlour concerts with it. But I wouldn't have any of it. I wanted *Bugle Call Rag* to be the tune that heralded our appearance. The fact that we were only piano and drums didn't deter me one bit. Anyway, he knew only half of *Here Comes Charlie* and none of *Bugle Call Rag* – and as I wouldn't play with him if he started off with *Here Comes Charlie* – we made a compromise and I opened our repertoire with a long drum solo. After my opening drum solo I was usually told in no uncertain terms to keep it down a bit; which in actual fact, really meant that's enough of that thank you.

The piano player knew only about a half of every tune, if that. He mostly knew the beginnings of tunes and some of the ends but seldom the middle. We sort of played seque – seque means playing about four or five numbers without stopping – but our kind of seque consisted of playing the beginning of one number and the end of a couple of others and perhaps a few more beginnings. Of course it confused people a lot when he played half of the beginning of one number, coupled with a half or a quarter of the end of another. When he did this I had to fill in quite a bit on the drums, despite the hostility to my percussive pieces.

The Syncopated Rhythm Boys were doomed not to go too far. Well they couldn't expand. Another instrument coming in would have introduced complexities too great for us to solve. The piano player could never have played with another instrumentalist unless he had learned to play in the same way; unless he also had known the beginnings, and the ends, and the parts of the middles of all the different tunes in the same order. No – it was fast becoming incumbent on me to ditch the piano player and move on with my drums into a higher musical sphere. You see in those days drummers were much sought after because what they were looking for was not so much someone who could play the drums, but someone who owned a drum kit; and the larger and more imposing the drums looked, the more sought after you became. The bigger the drum kit the bigger the band looked, and they liked to paint the name of the band on the big drum.

The first band I joined after ditching the piano player was a band called Howard Wynn-Jones and His Swingers, and we argued immediately over the band name. The others wanted it painted on the drums, to which I agreed, but I insisted that my name be on the drums too, but bigger, and above the band name, so that it would read 'JOHNNY SPEIGHT with Howard Wynn-Jones and His Swingers'. I thought it might be his band, but they were my drums ... and I wanted my name big.

Then we got the idea that the reason the band wasn't doing too well was because the drums didn't light up. It never entered our minds that it could be because the music was no good. It was because the drums didn't light up. So we drilled a small hole in the bass drum and threaded a piece of light flex through it. We took the skin out and put a bulb on the end of the flex, put the skin back and plugged the flex into a socket on stage and presto! ... the drum lit up ... with the name of the band on the front ... our telephone number ... palm trees ... and birds with naked bristols. One of the fellows was an artist . . . and still the bookings were hard to get.

We couldn't understand it. It wasn't a question of how good or how bad the band was. Nearly everyone in the area was tone deaf, the dancers had no ear for music, none of them had a feeling for rhythm even. I mean, they couldn't distinguish between a good band and a bad band – and we looked good. I had about the biggest set of drums in the area. I had the lot: swan neck cymbals, temple blocks, whistles, wood blocks, a tambourine for *The Galloping Major* and all that crap, castanets, maracas – I even had a football rattle for novelty effects. We just couldn't understand our lack of success. I mean, after all, my drum kit filled up quite a lot of the stage and made us look like a really big band. We'd even changed the name to Howard Wynn-Jones and His Big Broadcast Band and we really looked value for money. I even had six tom-toms which all lit up. They weren't real tom-toms. I couldn't afford the real thing. But what we did, one of the chaps worked in a factory where they used these cardboard drums for packing things in, and he'd nicked half a dozen, put legs on them, painted them and put lights in those as well. I couldn't play them but no one knew that. As far as the punters dancing round were concerned, there I was, manipulating this great wurlitzer of drums, with lights flashing on and off. It must have looked a fantastic spectacle.

We had music stands made. One of the lads was a carpenter and he made a good job of them. They looked really professional. The accordion player could read music and the alto player did a good job of appearing to. I had a stand also and made out to be reading all the weird crashes and bangs I was making. We had four extra music stands. Well – he had the wood over, so he thought he might as well knock them up, someone else might join us one day and if they did we had the stands ready. We used to put them out anyway, and it made us look like a bigger band where four musicians hadn't turned up. We got into trouble over it one night. The M. C. walked over, looked at the four extra music stands and said,

'Look, in future, when I book you ... everyone turns up, all right.'

And at the end of the evening, he only paid us half of what he'd promised us, saying,

'I'm not paying for a full orchestra when only half of you turn up.'

We weren't an exorbitantly priced outfit either. All we got normally was seven and six each and free tea and cakes.

Still, as far as we were concerned it was big money. It augmented our meagre earnings and we enjoyed doing it. We'd have done it for nothing and quite often did. We were the stars, the focal point of the evening; we were Howard Wynn-Jones and His Big Broadcast Band ... later on that was changed to Orchestra. Yes, we were a cut above those shitty-arsed wonders cavorting about the dance-floor. At one Town Hall they had a door round the back marked ... 'Artistes Only.' It was easier to go in the front way ... but that was the door I used. During the interval I used to walk out through that door for a smoke. I could smoke inside, but I was an artiste and I intended to take full advantage of my status. It was freezing cold standing in that doorway but I didn't mind. Above my head was a sign that said 'Artistes Only.' It made my day.

Our big ambition was to get uniforms. With uniforms we would really look something. Up until now we'd always worn white shirts with bow ties but they made us appear amateurish. I had a lounge suit which I'd dyed black and on which my sister had sewn black silk lapels. This suit, badly cut in the beginning and not tailored for me in the first place, but picked off the peg as the nearest size available, had not been improved by its conversion to evening attire. To say I cut a figure that was somewhat Chaplinesque hardly described my comic appearance. The trousers riding at least six or seven inches above my ankles did nothing to enhance the beat-up brown suede shoes with the thick crepe soles which were my pride and joy. And although fondly imagining it to be a mark of savoir faire to show a generous expanse of shirt cuff, the amount I had on show owing to my shrunken sleeves only added to the comic effect. But undaunted, until my reflection in a shop window gave me the gift to see myself as others saw me, I wore it on every possible occasion. The make do and mending I had to do to improve my appearance in those days. At one time I thought I was a dead ringer for Tyrone Power, if only my nose was uplifted, and I would stand for hours in front of a mirror, pressing it up with my finger. I still have a crease in it to this day. I even tried to get my hair to go black with coconut oil. I smothered it on because my father told me the lascars on the boats used it – and you never saw any of them with fair hair. (He also told me they cleaned their teeth with coal-dust, and wiped their arse with their right hand and a can of water. A kind of poor man's bidet.) I even took the added precaution of mixing it with boot black first. And one night going to the Hammersmith Palais it froze solid on the way to the bus stop, thawed out again on the bus; froze again while waiting for the train on Plaistow Station, thawed in the train and really melted in the Palais pouring down my face in black greasy streaks.

My musical colleagues resented me wearing my tux and complained that it gave the impression that I was the band leader. To which I replied that it didn't matter so much who appeared to be the band leader so long as somebody did, and that no useful purpose would be achieved by my dressing down to their standards but that, in fact, the reverse would benefit the band more.

This contretemps was eventually solved when we bought some old Army uniform mess jackets. They were blue with gold epaulettes and fitted us where they touched. Resplendent in these we practised feverishly, had cards and headed paper printed, and bought a microphone on hire purchase. The addition of the microphone must surely get us more bookings so we advertised thus: – Howard Wynn-Jones and his Big Broadcast Band – own MICROPHONE. With the arrival of the microphone we were now using quite a bit of electricity. What with the lights in the drums and the coloured fairy lights draped over the music stands – we had those now too – we had electrical leads plugged in all over the place and were in dire need of a full time electrician to work on maintenance. The guitarist had also decided that he was now some kind of crooner and was up at the mike

Boo-be-do-do-ing all over the place. The accordion player was a better singer but the guitarist argued that in every big band you ever saw on stage and films it was the guitarist who did the vocals. What we didn't realise was that they weren't guitarists at all, but singers, and rather than have them sitting on the end of the band twiddling their thumbs and looking out of place, the bandleader would give them a rubber stringed guitar to play. He was an awful singer our guitarist and the only way we could stop him doing his lousy impression of Bing Crosby was by playing numbers he didn't know, although his boo-be-do-dos covered up for a lot of missing words. His singing was made worse by the amplification system we were using, which was far from perfect, coupled with the acoustical defects prevalent in most town halls and the other places of entertainment that we played in. The people at the back of the hall would hear what we were playing about four bars behind what the people in the front were hearing, and those in the middle got a bit of each simultaneously. The sound was so bad that you would get a request for a number while you were actually playing it – but perhaps that was us. Quite a lot of the time I wasn't too sure what we were playing either. You know every band has a sound and I suppose if I were asked to describe our sound I would have had to say it was decidedly drummy, deafeningly so, with the almost discernible wail of a saxophone accompanied intermittently by an accordion. The insistent thump of the drums not only drowned the singer, it also made the rest of the band difficult to hear, which wasn't a bad thing. It also indicated the tempo of the number being played.

When I think of the time and energy that went into creating this awful noise, time and energy that could have been more profitably expended some other way; it's heartbreaking really to see people desperately struggling to be something they can never hope to be. Their vain attempts to scale the heights of their dreams giving glimpses of glorious high comedy to those who watch, but bringing them nothing but misery. Tragi-comedy is I suppose only funny to the really heartless. Does it purify our souls and make us think . . . there but for the grace of God go I? Or does it really make us feel self satisfied and superior to the poor

bastards it is happening to? I sometimes wonder. Our own musical tragi-comedy of that time brought no tears ... I suppose our
saviour was our ignorance. There is no real tragedy in being a fool
if you have no knowledge of being one. It is a bearable state, a
quite often happy state, until some clever bastard comes along
and opens your eyes to it. But even then ignorance ... complete
ignorance ... is a very protective shell ... the garb of idiots is hard
to crack open. Ours was never cracked open. We went on blithely
attempting to scale the heights of jazz. Our jazz equipment was a
few basic cowboy chords; we only knew a few notes and half of
those were wrong. The alto player as tone deaf as they come,
screwed his eyes into a look of concentrated rapture and squealed
his few painfully plaintive notes, the accordionist endeavoured to
create a pulsating drive with a few badly constructed block
chords, the guitarist scatter wailed into the microphone, and the
drummer belted furiously at everything within reach, and all of
them despising the thick clodhoppers shuffling about the floor in
front of them. They didn't dig our music man. It was soul de-
stroying having to play for these creeps. Here we were knocking
ourselves out for Christ's sake, giving them all we had. And all
these thick clots could do was shuffle about and talk to each other.
All right, the alto player was making a stinking mess out of *Ain't
Misbehavin'* – if that's what he was playing – and all right the
guitarist was no Louis Armstrong, but even Louis singing
through that microphone wouldn't have sounded much, and if he
had been singing through that microphone none of those cloth-
eared creeps would have known the difference anyway. All they
wanted was Victor Sylvester on bloody records ... with his perfect bloody tempo ... so that shitty arsed lot could do their
stiff-legged ballroom dancing ... Then over comes this brillian-
tined creep with the sideboards like Arthur English and wants
more waltzes – and can I keep the drums down a bit? It turns out
he's the M. C. and, 'Don't want any of that fucking coon music.'
His words. The alto gets into an argument with him and mentions
Harry Parry and his Radio Jazz Club or something ... and the
M. C. says,

'Sod Hari Kari,' and, 'We don't want no fucking Japanese

music either – just waltzes and foxtrots and less of the fucking drums. We're in a dance-hall,' he says, 'not in the fucking jungle.'

I say, 'Bollocks', quietly 'cos he's a big fellow and although he might look like a ponce he's probably a tough one. I get the wire brushes out and we play a waltz and we're all glad when that lot's over. And then some clot of a conductor won't let me bring the drums on his bus. It's raining and I can see that the others are all for pissing off and leaving me. Finally we have to lug the drums back into the hall and I have to get a day off from work and bring them home in instalments. I'm stopped a day's pay and it costs me three shillings out of my seven and sixpence in bus fares. My meagre wages are only augmented by four and sixpence that night. And thinking about it we didn't get any free cakes or tea that night either. We had to buy them from the bar at grossly inflated prices for what they were. But still our dreams of eventual fame and affluence never ceased although I was seriously considering leaving this crummy outfit. They were lousy musicians and although my drumnastic skills didn't merit much better, if they wouldn't help with the drums then to hell with them. I knew I might not find a better band to join up with at this stage in my career but, musical excellence aside, I might find one with some transport at least, or a few fellows more generous of spirit who wouldn't leave a chap on his own surrounded by drums at a bus stop. I mean, after all, the drums were a large part of our appearance, and they wanted all those tom-toms and lights as much as I did. I mean, they'd have looked nothing on all those Town Hall stages without my drums. And if I hadn't been so loud and busy on the drums people would have been able to hear them more clearly and then where would we have been? I covered a multitude of musical sins with my heavy handed rimshots. Their odd bits and pieces of tunes would have sounded pretty threadbare without me to fill in the gaps. They hardly knew a middle eight between them or where it went.

We were always on the look-out for pretty girls to sit in front of the band and sing a few numbers. We could find girls, some of them could sing a bit too, but we couldn't find one who could afford to buy a decent dress. And we wanted her dressed to kill. We didn't want her sitting up there in her working clothes. She had to look a bit above the girls who were dancing to us. We found one girl, the guitar player came up with her. He said she had two evening gowns, marvellous long legs and these great knockers. But when you finally got to her face all else was forgotten. She was so god awful ugly. I've always felt a bit sorry for ugly girls, they get a tough time, this one was in for a terrible time. A face like she had shouldn't be on a fellow even. They say God made us. Well, I don't know what He made her for. He probably had his reasons. But He didn't make her to sit in front of a band. We told her she could join the band as secretary and look after all the correspond-ence and what have you, provided she loaned her dresses to another girl we knew who was a real dish and could sing. Well, there were a few tears from the silly bitch, but as she was in love with the guitar player, and he didn't care what they looked like so long as he could bang them, everything turned out all right.

Once we got a black girl, a real kinky looking bird, she wasn't a bad singer either. She hadn't got a dance dress but we weren't bothered about that. We thought we'd take advantage of her colour and dressed her up in raffia skirts and put a lot of beads on her and one of those Hawaiian collars round her neck and got her to wriggle and dance barefoot. She had great legs and came over real sexy. So, we had an accordion and we converted the guitar with the aid of a piece of metal you slid along the strings to obtain an Hawaiian sound and told the sax to play reasonably straight but high pitched. I took the snares off and we became Howard Wynn-Jones and His Original Hawaiian Serenaders ... The music the natives love to hear. Of course the mess jackets and gold braid didn't fit this new Hawaiian image so we bought some cheap polo necks and sewed false buttons down one side of them from the neck and wore Hawaiian collars ourselves. We even toyed with the idea of blacking up. We had two bands now. Howard Wynn-Jones and His Big Broadcast Band, and The Original Hawaiians – and work was just as hard to get for either of them.

The accordion player was fast becoming a drag to us, he was

the only one who couldn't play by ear. Every new song that came out had him working three or four hours from a song copy before he could play anything that near resembled it. The alto's ear wasn't all that quick either and although the guitarist only had to strum he found it extremely difficult to strum in tune. They were so musically inept these three it was years before they could play *Tiger Rag* any faster than a waltz. I used to lose patience with them. By the time they were proficient enough to add a new number to our repertoire it was on the way out. Most of the time I wouldn't attend their practice nights. They gave me a pain in the arse with their doddering. I used to practise drum breaks on my own for as long as the family and neighbours would stand for it. I was a great fan of Joe Daniels and His Hot Shots in those days, and was always trying to get the band billed, 'Johnny Speight and His Hot Shots', but these other three squares wouldn't wear it. They preferred Howard Wynn-Jones and His Big Broadcast Band, or Howard Wynn-Jones and His Original Hawaiians.

It was my ambition to be known as the hottest drummer in Canning Town. There was another fellow billed as that already but I had four more cymbals than he had, two of them I couldn't use though, they were old hand-held cymbals with all the tone battered out of them. He played with a better band than I did which gave him a big edge. They played off professional band parts and, although I hated to admit it, they were all something a bit different to us. His father owned several big garages and transported the band everywhere – and with that kind of edge you don't need too much talent. Most people thought he was a lot better drummer than I was though, regardless of his father's transport, as the accordionist was always quick to point out. The accordionist didn't like me very much as I well knew, so he was naturally biased. But during more honest moments with myself, I had a nasty feeling that he was right, and that, unfortunately for the wellbeing of my ego, I was going to meet a lot of drummers who were a lot better than I was.

It's galling at times this having to admit, if only to yourself, the quite obvious superiority of others at something you dearly wish to excel in. Equality is all very well but it's useless if people will come along and insist on proving themselves superior. I mean, we all admire the man who can run a four minute mile, but if running a four minute mile is your only big claim to success, it's bloody infuriating if someone comes along who can run it in three. Your stock falls and you're a has-been to all those fat nothings who couldn't walk it in a day. No matter how much you lie and cheat about yourself, to yourself, or to others, when the chips are down and someone else scoops the board, it is a bitter moment. It's great to be the champion but usually, some place, somewhere, there's somebody just getting started who is going to overtake you. If you've got to lose, try and do it with elegance and grace. Some, with artful cunning, manage even to turn their defeats into victories. Statesmen and generals are particularly adept at this. It's much more difficult to do it in the arts, and impossible to do in sport, for there your defeat is clear to the most myopic of punters. In the arts, if your work sucks up to its audience and makes virtues out of its sins and evokes the smug, self-satisfied pleasure it seeks, then you will get applause, and plenty of back slapping, for the mediocre are the very first to applaud mediocrity.

Then I had a marvellous idea. I took the band's name off the drum. What happened was I needed a new skin because the one with the name of the band on it had exploded with the heat of the lamp. And so on the new skin I had painted ... JOHNNY SPEIGHT and HIS HOT SHOTS. Faced with this fait accompli they at last agreed we should form a third band. They had a round piece of cardboard cut to fit the drum with Howard Wynn-Jones and His Big Broadcast Band on one side, and on the reverse Howard Wynn-Jones and His Original Hawaiians. By the simple process of removing this card or turning it to either side we could show the name of the band we happened to be that evening. Sometimes the thumping on the drum displaced the card and despite what it should have been that evening the band became JOHNNY SPEIGHT and HIS HOT SHOTS for a short while. About this time I managed to get myself a caddie for my drums. He was a big rather gormless chap in many ways, a bit of a nutter I suppose, to carry all those drums without any thought, or even wish for reward. He was one of twelve kids living, two up two down, so there was obviously little or no comfort in his home. I doubt if there was even anywhere for him to sit down. He probably had to eat his meals standing up. I know they slept six to a bed.

Jazz had found a response in his soul the same as it had in ours, although the only soul that Jimmy was aware of in those days, and which caused him any discomfort, was the sole of his shoe. All the time I knew him the sole of at least one of his shoes leaked. However, I suppose he considered himself fortunate to have shoes, even leaky shoes, to worry about and give him discomfort. He'd run barefoot when he was younger, and even now his shoes had seen better wear on his brother's feet. As a child he'd always worn a long voluminous overcoat down to his ankles. People laughed at the length and misshapen size of this coat, but not Jimmy. It wasn't comic to him. To him that coat was God sent. Some days there was little but himself beneath it. I remember one hot summer, when the tar was melting on the roads and those lucky to have clothes had them sticking to them, Jimmy wore that coat although it must have been sweltering inside it. Jimmy knew though that if he once took that coat off he'd have the devil's own job getting it back on again, because there were six other kids in that family, near enough his size, who'd fight him for it and possession was nine points of the law. That coat was Jimmy's. It helped give him warmth when he needed it and he wouldn't risk taking it off for anything. Later on, when he was my drum caddie, he quite often left a dancehall wearing a better coat than the one he had entered with.

There was a trap-door in the shell of my bass drum which had been put there to facilitate the changing of the light bulb, and it was a long time before I became aware that it was being used as a booty sack for a lot of dance-hall loot. One night we kicked off with *Night and Day* and really began to sound like Ambrose with this loose cutlery effect. Jimmy had forgotten to empty the drum from a previous gig. And one night travelling home from a gig one of the lads complained that he was peckish and Jimmy opened the trap door of the bass drum and proceeded to dish out doughnuts, cakes, and sardines on toast. We were able to get on to buses much easier with Jimmy around. As I say, he was a big fellow, and although dim in most departments, he was far superior to an Einstein in a scrap. Fighting was where his ego found sustenance. The world around him could learn from his fists what he hadn't the words to convey. He felt equal to any man in this kind of debate. His ability to absorb pain would have won him A-levels if it had been an academic pursuit. I saw him batter men to the ground as a result of this quality alone.

Absorption of pain is a quality you need if you intend to get involved in a lot of fighting – ask any fighter. I mean, the idea is always to duck a punch, but if you've got to take one you had better be able to. I'm not saying he wasn't clever at it either, but no matter how clever a fighter you are, even the cleverest get hit, always assuming your opponent is roughly an equal, and Jimmy's always were. Most of them were bigger than himself. He was perverse enough to like them bigger. Bus conductors never yelled at him, 'You can't bring them drums on here!'

Big, burly, bruising Jimmy who really dug us, and genuinely believed we were as good as, if not better than, bands he heard on the radio. Well, he had one cauliflower ear, and his brain, scrambled as it was from jolting knuckles, could hardly be expected to accurately decipher what we were sending in through the other one. He couldn't play an instrument, but I don't think musical instruments meant much to him, only insofar as they were an accompaniment to the drums he adored. I used to let him sit in on the drums occasionally much to the annoyance of the rest of the band, but they were far too frightened to say anything, and he was like a child at Christmas, so excited he didn't know what to hit first, and then, suddenly, he would try and hit everything at once, playing havoc with the tempo.

I had cards printed with his name on; Johnny Speight and His Hot Shots – with Jimmy Nichols. He tried hard to persuade me to put his name on the drum as well. He managed to get a suit like ours not quite the same, but near enough, and sat at one of the spare music desks. He would carry my drums to wherever we were playing, put them all up, and then take up his position sitting with the band. I don't know what people thought; they used to look up at him and wonder what he was going to do – a juggling act? Or sing a song? He would have music in front of him which he'd turn over and gave the impression of I don't know what . . . When people stared up at him he would simply smile and nod to them . . . sitting there doing nothing . . . just beating time to the music with his feet, and turning his music over with the others . . . feeling as much a part of the band as they were.

'Johnny Speight and His Hot Shots – with Jimmy Nichols' looked good on the cards – it sounded like an added attraction. Jimmy would jump up and blow into the microphone, or tap it in the middle of a number to make sure it was working properly, causing a terrible whistling and thumping sound throughout the hall . . . Then he took it into his head to announce the numbers: 'Johnny Speight and His Hot Shots – with Jimmy Nichols' will now play for you . . . *Ain't Misbehavin'* and with a wave of his hand, 'Johnny Speight and His Hot Shots – with Jimmy Nichols!' 'A one-er . . . two-er . . . three-er . . . four-er . . . ' I got him to an-nounce, 'The . . . One and only Jimmy Nichols . . . '

Then the war broke out and put an end to the musical aspir-ations of Johnny Speight and His Hot Shots – with the one and only Jimmy Nichols and I never saw him again. And one gets the sad feeling that a Jimmy Nichols is the kind of chap who doesn't survive a war. Jimmy Nichols was the kind of chap who'd get talked into volunteering for a dangerous assignment very easily. Too easily I know he wouldn't have sat around with a blanket on or worn his uniform back to front. At the BBC if I see a band arriving and the drums being unloaded I look around to see if there's a big fellow . . . Well you never know, it's what he enjoyed doing most apart from fighting.

6 King George V and His Hot Shots – where my musical career is furthered by owning an instrument

When I was called up and posted to this semi-pro Army unit at Stratford East – although they don't actually post you in the G.P.O. sense (it means taking up your post) – they as near as dammit fix a tag round your neck and transport you like cattle to your destination. Here you are actually being coerced into giving your life for your country and they won't even go to a first class fare for you. The first thing they did was try and form a concert party. A notice appeared on the unit order board: 'Will all personnel able to play a musical instrument report to the entertainments officer.'

And when those of us who were musically gifted reported to take up our first military duties as musicians in H. M. Armed Forces we discovered that the only condition of acceptance was that of owning an instrument. I was promptly dispatched home for my drums, and on my return, a week later, a new name was affixed to my bass drum. Where it had read 'Johnny Speight and His Hot Shots,' it now read 'H. M. King George and His Hot Shots.' And while the mighty German fighting machine was busy girding its loins for battle, the only activity apparent in our unit was the attempt to form a dance band and get it into shape for a dance already advertised for the following Saturday night.

The pianist took over the leadership of this band on two counts.

First, he was a sergeant and the Adjutant's assistant and able to get us all relieved of guard duties and other chores equally distasteful, and secondly he was a really remarkable musician in comparison to the rest of us. He was wire-brush potty though and my incurable compulsion to play the drums busily and noisily drove him almost out of his mind. But alas, I was the only drummer in the unit, or rather the only drummer who also owned his own kit. This ideal state though wasn't to last, for very soon another much more accomplished drummer by far was to join us and become a nagging wretched pain in the arse to my ego. He had played in the West End with some of the best bands of the day and was all I dreamt of being. He was a really polished performer who played with 'light and shade' to quote our long suffering pianist; could read music, orchestrate, and actually play the piano, and was an even more accomplished musician than our leader, which got up his nose a little bit too.

Well, as you can imagine, the pianist wanted him, the band wanted him, the unit wanted him, but strangely enough he hadn't got a drum kit – there was some story or explanation attached to all this but I didn't bother to go into it. I think he'd flogged them or something when he was called up. Sufficient for me was the fact that he hadn't got one and I had and I was no democrat. Of course, I was shamed into letting him play a few numbers, and made to look silly when he did one of his almost Gene Krupa like drum solos and the crowd stopped dancing to gather round the stand to watch him. Furious hardly describes my feelings. I felt pretty sick and humiliated, especially when the rest of the band got to buying me free drinks to keep me in the bar and off the drums. I must say, this drummer was pretty decent about it, but he could afford to be. I mean, he had the hero's part. He was the stinking good guy. And when he was finished and everyone was clapping and cheering their silly heads off, he'd stand up and give this phoney bow, he wasn't a bit humble really, he was a bloody snob really, but he'd stand there bowing this phoney bow and everybody screaming out for more, and then he'd get all modest and shake his head, and beckon me over, and hand me the sticks and climb down off the stand to more wild cheers, leaving me up there like a great big ninny, and I wouldn't be able to play for fury, and anyone who was a bit decent, feeling sorry for me I suppose. I know I felt bloody sorry for me. I felt bloody depressed and lousy for me. I hate it when I'm made to feel sorry for myself. I'd much rather feel sorry for other people. But I had no chance with this goon. I suppose I acted very much like a Tory over this situation, they were my drums, I had the undisputed right of ownership which I wouldn't relinquish. I was the man of property, the fly in the ointment, the reactionary holding back the natural progress of the band, the one standing between it and this more brilliantly gifted drummer. It made me feel very petty, but it didn't make me change my attitude. One of the most galling things about all this was that I used to practise regularly for long hours at a stretch, while he never practised at all. He even scorned the need of it, and preferred to spend his spare time drinking, or with girls. Which brought home to me quite painfully that effort alone is not always enough. He even slept in a field all night with a girl I had been going out with, and who I hadn't dared even to kiss. It was a hateful period all round, and brought home to me quite forcibly, that nature is haphazard in the way it distributes talent and that there is no way of earning it no matter how one tries.

Anyway, all this was brought to a head by the entertainments officer suddenly deciding to buy a new set of drums for the unit. This move wasn't inspired purely to get rid of me, my drums were getting old and battered, and I suppose, it was fascinating to wonder how good this new drummer would sound on a really super modern new kit of drums. And this is what they bought. They even gave me weekend leave to take my drums home and dump them there at my own expense. They even allowed me to play a few numbers at the dances. This was obviously at the magnanimous suggestion of their new wizard of the skins so that he could nip into the bar and down a few and chat up the birds. I should have told them to piss off but my love of the drums was greater than my pride.

I didn't know it at the time but this period was to be turned to good use. When you mix with the great a lot can rub off, providing you are intelligent enough to absorb it. Life is strange at times, and what, at a certain moment in time, can only be regarded as terrible misfortune, and bitter experience, can also be viewed in retrospect as a happening of great benefit in the long term. So it was with me, getting the boot out of the band in favour of this other drummer. For, as I have said, he was a really good drummer, a top liner who had played in several name bands, and the kind of first class professional who I would have given a lot to meet under normal circumstances, and talk to, and learn from. Which I did. And although at first I resented his ability, which had wounded my vanity, and threatened my joyful and carefree way of life as the unit drummer, as soon as I lost the job I was thrown into the wearisome whirl of guard duties, cookhouse fatigues, early morning P. T. and parades ad nauseam, and all the rest of the military bullshit the musicians were exempt from due to the late hours they suffered playing at the various and many dances. The late hours suffered! They were a ball.

Once the situation was clarified we became good friends and he taught me an awful lot, and my near hatred of him was transformed into unstinting admiration, and we could always be found in some corner of the billet tapping out rhythms and executing breaks and talking drums tirelessly. We worked out a drum routine together, and rehearsed it to perfection, and one night we did it on stage . . . and it went a bomb, we really tore the place up, and had them stamping, applauding, and screaming for more. It was a great routine and looked as good as it sounded, the other drummer was doing all the really clever stuff, all the more intricate rhythms, but to the less discerning it was difficult to tell who was doing what.

The praise was like strong wine to my ego, I was drunk with glory as people came up to me and with adulatory pats on the back, asked me why I didn't play more often, and I gave them a lot of phoney modesty about standing down for a better man and a lot of crap like that. But managing the impression that I was one of those really good guys who was really genuinely above the kind of petty squabble about who was best, and all that vanity shit, and that if certain people thought he was better – well . . . there wasn't that much in it . . . and that he was also a very talented guy . . . and that any kind of shabby, knife in the back stuff, didn't suit my kind of wonderful integrity . . . But I never went on like this if he was around. While in his presence I was so sycophantic he was embarrassed into ludicrous praise of me . . . Which is funny really, because I didn't intend to be that clever, unwittingly producing an effect that had me blushing with ill-concealed pleasure . . . and put me in a better light than all the shifty crap I'd been dishing out. And had me looking like the real old shiny reticent hero . . . like Tyrone Power with a blood-stained bandage round my head, a little white and drawn with a wan smile, but brave – brave beyond measure.

My fantasies always took the shape of one of those lousy romantic films with me derring doing all over the place. In my favourite, the one I re-ran all the time, I was a spy for H. M. Government, the greatest spy they'd ever known, but for reasons of security my heroism must be concealed from those who scorned me, no hint of my amazing bravery could be indicated. My favourite scene had the heroine learning who I was after just having given me a white feather and declaring her contempt for me.

I must have been a right little masochist. I used to get completely immersed in my day dreams. Well, my inner world was far better than my outer world, it was a gayer, more fascinating world and I was its star. I would walk around oblivious of the people about me, bashing into them, and causing motorists to hoot as I almost walked under their wheels. I'd even pass family in the street and not notice them. They all thought I was a bit simple. Well, I suppose you couldn't blame them, I would genuflect to the conductor getting on to a bus and make the sign of the cross before I handed him my fare, they weren't to know that in my mind this wasn't a bus and that I was actually having an audience with the Pope, discussing with him, at his own request, how best to defend the Vatican against the horde of cannibal Protestants hammering on the gates. My mother thought I had habits and kept dragging me around to all these different doctors in all these different hospitals. And she would get annoyed because I wouldn't do my habits for them. And she'd say, 'Go on. Do your habits for the doctor.' And when I wouldn't do them, she'd give me a poke and say, 'He won't do 'em now. He was doing 'em all the way up on the bus.' I'd just sit there and say nothing. Looking surly, sullen, and I suppose, bloody stupid. But how do you explain, especially to a cold fish of a doctor, that the weird gesticulations I made were nothing more than the outward manifestations of my inner fantasy world?

Anyway, I was very wary of hospitals and hospital people in those days, especially wary of the Harley Street specialists who walked their wards. I had been told that these rich Harley Street specialists only came down to the East End to practise on the poor. That made sense to me. They couldn't afford to risk the lives of their wealthy patients – it wasn't good business. The loss of a rich patient would be a nasty blow to their bank balance, but a dozen poor people was no skin off their nose at all. I was told that if you hadn't got a disease they gave you one, so they could have a go at curing it. Well, surgery was becoming very fashionable in those days, and some of these Harley Street specialists were very quick to get the knife out in the East End. I heard of people going into hospital with a bad arm and ending up having a leg off.

I know of one fellow who had an operation, and he had to go back a week later to be opened up again – this bloody surgeon had left half his tools inside him. There are some people even today in the East End who don't trust hospitals. Well, the way they work it out is I suppose that people are better to practise on than monkeys, and poor people are cheaper than monkeys. It's not so far fetched – Hitler's doctors were at it, weren't they? And when I was a kid in Canning Town the poor people weren't a lot better off than the Jews were under Hitler. And I'll tell you another thing, if this transplant business makes any real headway it could become dangerous for a poor person to go into hospital because they might start nicking parts off them. I mean, there could be a market for those rather similar to the Nazi lampshade market in Germany. Our muggers as yet are not as bad as the muggers of the Seven Dials district of yesteryear. Then, they not only mugged you, they sold your body as well. And who to? Why, the brass-plated gentlemen of the medical profession. And of course there was Burke and Hare – they almost became as big as Marks and Spencers.

Shortly after that, I was posted to a unit who had a band whose drummer was not as good as I now was. The roles were now reversed and it was my turn to take over. I had learned a lot from my usurper. He was the first one to convince me that a drummer also had to be a musician. This fact had never occurred to me before. Up until then I had worked on the assumption that only the others had to know about music, and all I had to do was chip in with what I thought fitted. This I still did, but now I'd discovered that it worked better if I listened to what the others were playing. This was easier too, because now the others were also musicians.

This band consisted of drums, piano, double bass, trumpet, and tenor and alto sax, and we could play small band arrangements and make sense. We were very danceable to, very jazzy, and also fast becoming something of a showband. I also did unto this other drummer what had been done unto me by the drummer who had taken over from me. I sat in with this new band when I first arrived and went through every trick in the book that I had learned from my erstwhile friend. I was given an ovation at the end; found myself doing everything that he used to do, the phoney bow, the modest smirk ... God, it was sick-making to see myself doing it and be powerless to stop it. What a creep I was. Here I was doing to somebody else exactly what I'd hated this drummer for doing to me. I didn't take his girl into a field all night though. I might have done if she hadn't been so bloody ugly. Anyway, it was winter, and I didn't fancy taking any girls into any fields in that part of icy, dreary, bloody silly Suffolk.

I was also doing a bit of writing without being aware of it. I was organising the showband side of the outfit, and found that more and more they were calling on me to organise a complete concert. I had even worked out an act for myself. It wasn't original. I'd seen it done before. But in those days I believed that all art was a stream and you dipped your bucket in and took out what you needed. So I painted my drum sticks and a pair of gloves with luminous paint and played my big drum solo using these with the hall plunged into darkness. It was a gas, it looked so effective. It gave the impression of a disembodied pair of hands playing an invisible drum kit.

I remember the first time I did it was at Diss in Norfolk, and the natives thought I was some kind of witch doctor I'm sure. They were flabbergasted. They'd never seen such magic. It stopped the show. They gathered round, all these yokels with straw sticking out of their hair. I tell you, I could have formed a new religion there and then, no bother. For an encore I played the drums again, still with luminous sticks and gloves, on to the rims of the drums, all along the floor, up the wall, and then I'd throw the sticks into the air and they would vanish behind a screen that stood behind me . . . a pause pregnant with silence as the sticks vanished . . . and then we'd let a shower of luminous sticks fall from the ceiling . . . about a hundred of them . . . and in the darkness they made a wonderful effect . . . looking like a shower of luminous sticks of lightning . . . or long slivers of ice . . . or what-ever the yokels imagined them to be . . . they were a thick bunch. All the intelligent ones had been called up. What was left was really ripe for the three-card trick.

We also had a hunchback in this band who sang a bit like Frank Sinatra. How he got into the Army I'll never know. The M. O. who passed him must have been as blind as a bat. Anyway, this hump made him look more like Sinatra than even Sinatra looked in those days. He was thin like Sinatra and not unlike him to look at, what you could see of him. He would drape himself over the microphone and give out with a current Sinatra, and the likeness was uncanny. His surname was Reed but he insisted on being billed as Simatra – Frankie Simatra. The unit was willing to spend some money on the band, well we were entertaining the troops and the locals, so we bought him a suit and had the jacket made about four sizes too large in an endeavour to make the hump look more like round shoulders. (Some American soldiers who had actually seen Sinatra told us that Sinatra's hump was round shoulders and not a deformity.)

Christ, he really looked more like Quasimodo. He bent his

knees as he imagined Frank Sinatra did and people thought he was a cripple. I heard one chap say, 'He don't sing bad for a hunchback, do he?' Some peope thought he was a comedy act, some people thought he was for real, but they all liked him for whatever reasons. A lot of the girls went crazy about him. Well, he was probably the first live entertainment they'd seen in that area. And watching him was better than watching the bacon slicer. This kind of thing was first class material to them. They had no variety halls in the area, no telly to compare with, and their radio sets, the few that had them, were so cheap and so old that I suppose even Frank Sinatra must have sounded pretty awful to them.

He was a great character this one. Everyone was impressed with the Americans in those days. We'd been brought up on American movies. And Frankie, I don't know what his real name was, it might have been Frankie for all we know, he was a pack of lies anyway, had this marvellous American accent. When I first met him I thought he was an American, he took terrible liberties with his uniform. He wore a pair of American olive drab slacks, an army battledress top, and an American forage cap out of camp. He really diced with the Military Police. He sometimes went out wearing an American officer's uniform that he'd got from somewhere. There was an American unit stationed near us and he was always in their camp. He was happier with them than he was with us, except for a few of us, and smoked Lucky Strikes or American cigars. His American accent was a lot better than that of most Americans, or at least the American soldiers we met. His accent was closer to the way they spoke in American films and on the American Forces Network. He never spoke in that slob, ugly way, the way most Americans speak.

He got on to the band truck one night with this American officer's uniform on – U. S. Army badges on, the lot. And when we got to this camp we were playing we were met by their entertainments officer who asked Frankie if he was an American. I thought, 'Here we go, trouble from the off.' But Frankie spoke to him in his own English voice, the voice he'd been brought up with and it was cockney, terrible cockney almost as bad as mine.

Obviously like me he'd never worked on it the way he'd worked
on his American voice, and said to the officer,

'No sir. I wear this in the act. It's props like. See, I didn't know
what the er . . . changing conditions would be like here see . . . and
I didn't want to have to change on the truck like . . . You know.'
And he got away with it. But to everyone else that night he was an
American on loan to 'these cock-sucking limeys . . . to jazz up their
cock-sucking concert party.'

I heard him talking to some bird, and the patter he was giving
her . . . 'Yeah, I saw Bing afore I left the States . . . I was doing a
charity with him. Yeah, the old groaner's still croaking 'em . . .
Yeah, we're good friends . . . Jesus baby . . . there's no competition
there . . . we're a different age group . . . ' And to a fellow behind
the bar, 'Sorry, that's a dollar baby . . . just a minute . . . I got some
goddam limey money here some place . . . ' He always had these
dollar bills. To him they were stage money.

It was a good outfit we had though. Apart from Frankie Simatra, we had an alto player who did a very powerful imitation of
Benny Goodman; the piano player was no mean hand, the bass,
tenor and trumpet were well above average, and I was improving
all the time. Yes, in our opinion, we were ready for the radio and
the high life. But there was a bloody war on!

I must say here though that I don't regret one moment of the
war. It was the first time in my life that I had a bed to myself. It
was also a kind of university to me, a time and place of real
learning. I am not saying that to experience the holocaust of war
is a necessary concomitant to learning. It is inclined to speed the
process though; living that close to death and destruction, dirt,
butchery, and boredom. Clearly evident on all sides too was the
lunatic assumption that a public schoolboy was better fitted to
lead men into action than a plater's mate. From my experience
the average N. C. O. was much better equipped on a battlefield
than the average officer, and most Regimental Sergeant Majors
ran their units. But we quite often had to take orders from an
obvious fool whose only claim to superiority was a comic accent
and a loafish adolescence. Of course they were forced to com-
mission lots of N. C. O.s as the war dragged on, and these became

harder task masters and much more efficient officers than their public school counterparts. Look around our present day society and you will find many men of working class origins in high positions of power and affluence. Unfortunately many of them are insensitive, selfish, money-grubbing bastards lacking in all the common decencies, and without even the table manners of the aristocracy who preceded them.

Anyway, the war ended, I was demobbed with a cheap ill-fitting suit, and was back on the factory circuit once more. I wanted very much to become a professional drummer now but no professional bandleader thought me worthy of hire. I couldn't read music you see and during the big band era a drummer who couldn't read was useless. Having a drummer who couldn't read in a band was rather like having an actor in a play who didn't know his part. I began to study music but I had a long way to go and people now were flooding out of the Army, and it seemed to me that most of them were drummers. I was doing plenty of auditioning. Some weeks I managed as many as seven or eight auditions.

I remember arguing with my parents, 'What d'you mean I'm not getting anywhere? I've had more auditions this week than I've ever had.' One audition I had was with a band of dwarfs and the leader told me that he liked my drumming but he couldn't fit me in because I was too tall. I was choked. I felt like saying to him, 'I don't fit? It's you lot who don't fit. You're too small.' I had tea with them after the audition and they poured out all their troubles to me. Troubles like how difficult it was to get furniture to fit them. One of them told me his wife had to stand on a chair to turn the gas stove on; and they both had to stand on the lavatory seat to pull the chain. They were having a real moan about kitchen sinks and gas stoves and whatnot . . . they wanted to know why the gas company and the water board couldn't convert children's kitchen toys into the real thing for dwarfs. They certainly had a point and a problem. Although I found it hard to turn on too much sympathy for them. Well, they had a solid year's theatre bookings and all I had was the Assistance Board. You know, it was one of those ironies, if I'd been three feet smaller there was a job staring me in the face. I mean, it wasn't their musical ability that was getting them the work – it was their size. They were nice people though and they said they were terribly sorry that I wasn't three feet smaller.

I had a row with this pimply faced goon at the Assistance Board the next day. I still hadn't got a job and told him I needed more money.

'All right,' he yelled, 'so you fought in a war. I fought in a war. Everyone's fought in a war. Now everyone's trying to get a job. Why don't you try and get a job?'

I said, 'I could have got a job if I'd been a bloody dwarf!'

Christ, he was tight. I was always rowing with him about money. I said to him,

'Look, I only want a few bob for the pictures, for Christ's sake!'

You'd have thought it was his own money the way he went on. I said to him,

'Look, pimples,' I said, 'if it wasn't for people like me you wouldn't have a job.' And then I tried to explain to him.

'Gene Krupa's on at the Odeon,' I said, 'and if I go and study him for a few days it's going to improve my drumming, right? And if I improve my drumming it could lead to a job, couldn't it? And if I get a job I won't have to come down this crap hole anymore, will I?' But he wasn't very bright.

'All right,' I said, 'I need the money to get to Manchester. I've been offered a job there.'

'What job?' he said.

'Brain surgeon,' I said.

Well, you tell them the truth, that you want the money to go to the pictures and they turn nasty. I discovered it was lies that got the best results. So after a while I got to telling them that I needed the money for fares and things so I could look for work. They had to be really dopey if they thought I was going to waste the money they gave me looking for work. No, the front row of the cinema gazing up at the silver screen was more to my liking. I went most of the day without much to eat but there was always a bed at home and an evening meal for a fellow who had supposedly tramped the streets all day looking for work.

I was always round at the doctor's too, acting out my various symptoms to him. I was helped here by a very pallid complexion and a frail physique. Also by the fact that he wasn't a very good doctor. He was one of the old two bob a visit and coloured water quacks. A lot of those did well out of the National Health Service. How this one ever became a doctor I'll never know. His father was one of the old medicine men, who after a long and illustrious career as a fairground practitioner, had set up shop in the back room of a secondhand clothes dealer, where, apart from brewing his own special brand of cure-all potions, had also bred leeches for his more fashionable colleagues. He had obviously inherited a lot of his father's fairground magic because people swore by his cochineal and water remedies.

His waiting room was a filthy dirty, draughty, depressing hovel, full of people passing around their germs and the last place to sit in if you were really ill. In fact when the government brought in the National Health Scheme and people began to get a reasonable sickness benefit those who wanted a few weeks off with pay used to go and sit in his waiting room and hope to catch something. He kept a good supply of old comics and periodicals there and quite a few people used it as a reading room. Before the National Health Scheme you had to show him your two bob before he'd do business with you. He wouldn't give credit under any circumstances, obviously he never had as much faith in his potions as his patients had. On a night call you would have to pass the money through his letter-box before he'd come out. In fact, he'd look out of his bedroom window and you'd have to shine a torch on the money before he'd come downstairs even. Shaw writes somewhere about an uncle of his who was forced by circumstances to trade with the poor and used to insist on his night patients rattling their money at the speaking tube by his front door. He worked on the principle that if you died it was the will of the Lord, and if you recovered he took the credit. It was all a bit hit and miss. Before the National Health Scheme began he'd fob you off with a bottle of his pink or purple special, whichever was the colour of the day. But once the National Health Scheme was in operation he had to write out prescriptions and quite often the chemist couldn't decipher them so you would have to describe your symptoms all over again to the chemist and he'd give you what he thought was best. It was usually pink or purple water. But he was always good for a doctor's certificate and that was all I wanted.

Still, he brought a lot of them into the world, kept their kidneys flushed with his coloured water while they lived, and was prompt with a death certificate so that the bereaved could collect the insurance money quickly, and touted for at least one undertaker on the side. I always thought he should have had an ostrich feather stuck in a band round his head and worn a bone through his nose. He was our Ju-Ju man. By the way, if it was a cold day and you wanted to warm yourself by the broken gas fire in his waiting room you had to put your own penny in the meter and light it yourself.

And the dentist who kept shop four doors down the road used to work in a sound-proof room. He had two prices – with or without gas. I go to a dentist in Wimpole Street now who puts you to sleep in a booklined room furnished with antiques, you don't see his chair. He even puts gold fillings in false teeth. It's a different life.

7 Moss Side Manchester

I travelled around a lot playing the drums. Have drums, will travel. That was me. I very seldom played in the same place twice, or with the same band. I was booked into Manchester at one time. I was offered this job in Archer Street. Playing at a jazz club in Manchester for two pounds ten a night. I borrowed the fare and went up on a coach. Found myself some digs for thirty shillings a week in some crappy place called Ebberley Hall, that stank of boiled cabbage and cats' piss. It was a bit like Rowton House (the Rowton Houses were a chain of hostelries for tramps. I think Conrad Hilton bought the original sites and transformed them into concrete blocks of plastic bedrooms for the rich). The room had a bed, a chair and a table, a gas ring and a window with a piece of dirty cloth hanging across it. I can't give a better description of it than that. Nobody could. The wallpaper was some colour or the other . . . if it was wallpaper . . . It was peeling anyway but then paint peels. I know there was no bulb in the light and every day I was promised one but I never got it. But I wasn't bothered about the light bulb – it wasn't the kind of room you wanted to see anyway.

I had just arrived and Manchester to me had an air of mystery and glamour about it. I didn't expect to be ensconced in the Midland Hotel – not yet anyway. I was fully employed as a jazz drummer and nothing, not even this gloomy refuge for homeless bugs, could dampen my spirits or take the joy out of my life at this moment. Fully employed! I was yet to discover that I was to be fully employed for one night a week only. And that after paying for my digs I was to be left with only a pound to spend, and seven long days in which to spend it. Jesus. I must have been mad. But I stuck it out. Mainly because I hadn't got the fare home.

I remember, I wrote to a friend of mine, an alto player, and described my life and times in Manchester in such glowing terms, giving an impression of such wild success and bacchanalian nights, that he withdrew his savings and came up on the next bus, providing me with a lodger, an extra pound a week and a companion to share my misery with. I don't think he minded too much though. He was a pretty casual sort of guy and usually made the best of wherever he was, and after a good moan about all my lies he settled down to enjoy what he could of it. Which wasn't much. He took a shine though to an out-of-work prostitute who was living across the passage from us, and although he was near enough penniless and far from the average girl's dream of a sex symbol, they knocked up a kind of sexual alliance – she needed to keep her hand in I suspect. I was a little worried in case he moved in with her and I lost my quid a week rent. But I had nothing to fear on that score, his morals, such as they were, forbade him living with a prostitute. They didn't prevent him banging her regular though (and regular they were – they banged round the clock).

I had the room to myself almost, he only used it to change his shirt and practise his saxophone in. He also had this idea he should get all the sex practice he could in case he ever married. And he had it figured he would get a higher standard of coaching from a professional than he would get from an amateur. He had no regard for amateurs in any field. He really was bugged on this idea of sex practice. I don't think he enjoyed sex with this prostitute. He regarded it more as a workout to keep himself match fit for Mrs Right, if and when she came on the scene. He married a pro in the end. A girl with a fine track record gained from a list of well paid events in Maddox Street. They were married in white at the Brompton Oratory and the reception at Claridges sported some of the finest names from Debrett and Archer Street. The last I heard they were running a chain of respectable middle-class brothels in the Midlands, and arranging champagne wife-swapping parties at Ascot and Newmarket. At least all those marathon training sessions at Ebberley Hall weren't wasted on some lousy amateur.

Apart from my one night stand in this jazz club, the alto player (Peter Green his name was) and myself had successfully canvassed a few more dates on Moss Side, a black ghetto in Manchester. We were still poor and not yet above looking in butcher's shop windows to decide on whether to buy a pork pie or two penn'orth of chips. One day we spent an hour discussing a menu like this until we finally succumbed to the smell of the chip shop. Moss Side, as far as it existed for us, was four tatty night clubs and a barber's shop. The barber's shop was the centre of the Hip community ... where it all happened. And there, apart from getting your barnet tonsorially splendoured – some of these black cats spent small fortunes on their woolly heads – you could wise-up on the racing news, the local birdery and purchase the various brands of boot-legged marijuana. It was a bit like how I always imagined Harlem to be. Peter and I really dug it there. It was our scene. I was really getting educated. I was really learning 'a way of separating the straight people from the squares and cripples' to quote Billie Holliday. My philosophy in those days was more or less contained in the sardonic lyrics of *God Bless the Child*.

> Them that's got shall get
> Them that's not shall lose
> So the Bible says
> And it still is news
> Mama may have
> Papa may have
> But God bless the child that's got his own
> That's got his own.

Yes, the strong gets more
While the weak ones fade
Empty pockets don't
Ever make the grade
Mama may have
Papa may have
But God bless the child that's got his own
That's got his own.

Money, you've got lots of friends
Crowding round your door
But when it's done
And spending ends
They don't come no more
Rich relations give
Crust of bread and such
You can help yourself but don't take much
Mama may have
Papa may have
But God bless the child that's got his own
That's got his own.

Bernard Shaw was alive in those days and I was always reading some remark of his in the newspapers. They were always very funny and I imagined him a stand-up comic like Tommy Trinder, and I thought I must catch his act one day. Then, looking in Canning Town Public Library for something to read, I saw this shelf of books and I thought, 'Christ. He writes as well.' The first book of his I read was *Immaturity*, a novel. Reading Shaw was to me at that time, I suppose, as near as one could get to a kind of divine revelation. It was as though a light had been turned on and every dark recess lit by sweet reason, or like coming up against cool, clear sanity in a madhouse. The whole of life was made to look brighter and more hopeful than ever before.

Since reading Shaw I have come into contact with other great writers, dramatists, philosophers, economists, thinkers, poets and advocates, and hawkers of all manner of philosophies and ways of life, but none has influenced me more, or made the same impact on my mind that Shaw did. If God could write he couldn't write better than Shaw. The mystery of life is a mystery to all of us but the lunacies it is prone to are shown nowhere better than in the works of Shaw.

I did most of my early reading in the public library; the whole of Shaw, Chekhov, Strindberg, Wilde, O'Casey, Ibsen, Marx – not Groucho, he hadn't written any books yet, he was probably still in Vaudeville – Wells, Shelley, Keats, William Morris, Samuel Butler and a host of others. Naturally, I did my best to boost their royalties by making sure quite a few of their books got lost, forcing the library to buy new copies to replace them. When I say lost, I'm using the old East-End term meaning stolen. No, that's a hard term, stolen. Borrowed. It was a lending library and I borrowed their books for a much longer period than most. They had a fining system for long borrowers, but if you were too poor to pay, which I always pleaded, because I always was, they didn't bother.

What was the alternative, nick, at their expense? And a bit of hard labour that was less hard, probably, than what I was doing already? Punishment by imprisonment is a funny old business. I've always thought it a bit unequal, perhaps unfair is a better word. It's worse punishment for a rich respectable person to be sent to prison than it is for a poor and unruly person. For some poor people, tramps in particular, prison can be a step up the social ladder, and a lot more comfortable than sleeping in a draughty doorway. And for the criminal classes it's almost home from home, and better perhaps. A good many of their friends and relations are there already, or should be, if the police were doing their job properly, whereas the more affluent and better brought up are made to suffer much more by being deprived of their greater creature comforts.

Another piece of philanthropy I practised in those days was while working for the Performing Rights Society, a body responsible for earmarking royalties to composers. Cards were given to us clerks itemising the song titles and compositions played, and our job was to add the composer's name to the work in question to enable the Society to pay the royalties due. Well, my musical tastes were very biased in those days, they probably still are. I had my favourites who were mostly jazz men, and when there was doubt about the origins of a piece, Charlie Parker or Count Basie, Louis Armstrong or Duke Ellington got the benefit. The royalties for *Greensleeves*, I know, went mostly to Charlie Parker. This was how a number of jazz musicians came to be earning out of Beethoven and Mozart. I told Stan Getz this story and he said,

'Get back in the job, we need you.'

Speaking of Stan Getz, he told me that when he joined the Benny Goodman band he was provided with a band suit that was four sizes too large for him. When Stan pointed this out, Benny Goodman said,

'Don't worry about it, you'll be sitting behind a music stand, just roll your sleeves up, nobody'll notice.'

'But what about when I stand for my solos?' Stan said. 'My pants will fall down.'

'Don't stand for your solos,' Benny said, 'stay seated. Look, we're making a film in a few months, and the studio will kit us out. No sense buying a new band suit for you just now.'

Anyway, Stan stayed seated to play his solos and got the reputation of being real cool. Being the great tenor sax he was, he was soon copied by other saxophone players who admired him and wished to emulate his style.

On Moss Side now Peter Green and I were really getting ourselves a night club tan. We were doing about three or four nights a week in the clubs there, and becoming very popular. We got on well with the black population of Moss Side. I have never been able to understand people who consider themselves superior genetically to black people, or any other people for that matter, but Peter Green was the other way, he preferred them and would have liked to have been one. Here was a white lad, grammar school educated, who would rather have been born black and resented the fact that he wasn't. He envied black people, more especially the American negro, their jazz environment. They were born with a natural feeling for jazz, a feeling he had to work hard at emulating. There was a black boy we used to stay with on

Moss Side, Snowy was his name, a real jazzy character, who polished his floor by shuffle dancing on a couple of dusters to jazz records.

There were a lot of American Army negroes on Moss Side in those days, and Peter couldn't understand the enmity that existed between them and the British blacks. He loved them all and could see no harm or evil in any of them. Even when one of them sold him a twist of Brooke Bond tea leaves for a fiver, in place of marijuana, he bore no resentment. Anything they did was all right by him. He told me the only reason he liked my drumming was because I had a black beat. He met up with a black whore in one of the clubs we were playing and bought up all of her time so he would have a black chick for a girlfriend. He was paying her something like a pound a night to have her sit and watch him play the alto. He got a tremendous kick out of this, but it was costing him every penny he earned and he was starting to put the bite on me. And because I wasn't too keen to subsidise this strange affair he accused me of being a racist, and we started to fall out. I had to get Snowy to try and talk some sense into him. Snowy tried to persuade Peter to give her up but he wouldn't hear of it and so Snowy who, it turned out, had quite a business flair, managed to talk Peter into allowing him to sublet her for part of the evening. Peter, thus reimbursed, I was able to get him off my back. I discovered later that Snowy had managed to get a far better price for Peter's girlfriend than Peter was paying her and had naturally pocketed the difference. Also, this profitable venture on Peter's behalf had opened his big brown eyes to a new and more lucrative way of life and without further ado he moved into the girlie business in a big way and even found work for Peter's other penurious prostitute friend, the one living across the passage from us at Ebberley Hall, curtailing Peter's grisly practice sessions a bit but getting the poor girl off her back and on to her feet (by way of getting her on to her back more profitably, I suppose) in fine style. Just before we left Moss Side, Snowy, not one to forget old friends, was driving us on gigs in a huge, showy limousine.

Snowy had no hang-ups about living off the immoral earnings

of the girls he managed and, I suppose, his immoral earnings were no more immoral than the earnings of the average employer of labour on Moss Side. Besides, he managed their affairs much better than they could themselves, vetting prospective customers, not so much for their desirability as for their solvency or willingness to pay for the voluptuous eroticisms supplied, and sorting out and grooming the more personable and attractive of them, the more comely and seductive, for the better pickings their rented charms merited, but always maintaining a rate for the job commensurate with the odious allure of the ill-favoured, hard-faced, scraggy majority. Gazing on some of the dregs that Snowy represented I was hard put to imagine what peculiar attraction they could hold for anyone. Perhaps it was my Irish heredity or some puritanical streak in my nature that I could always see more value for money in a bottle of Scotch than the dubious pleasures these scrofulous young hags had to offer. But there were some who found solace in their company and paid well over the odds for it in my opinion. I preferred masturbation myself, a do-it-yourself sexual practice that ensures you always keep the best possible company; an inexpensive sexual pursuit that appeals to the thrifty, and makes it enormously popular in Scotland. Hence, the wearing of the kilt, a garment designed obviously for a quick one off the wrist.

You can't blame some of these girls going on the game though. After all, their environment doesn't fashion them for much more in the way of a career than whoring, or long hours of wearing drudgery in the local paint factory, or spring-clip lacquering, or some other monotonous, mind-dulling task; or perhaps marriage to some lad with an equally futile future sentenced to a lifetime of hard labour with living quarters in one of our modern slums which, let's face it, are nothing more than open prisons. No wonder some of these chaps come home drunk and beat up their long suffering wives, and smash up all the crockery in the house. It's surprising they stop at that.

8 Clacton, or further adventures with food, and where I meet the wandering Heifetz

I went to Clacton-on-Sea on spec with this same alto player. We had no work to go to but then we had no work in London to go to either, and we reasoned that if you are going to starve you may as well starve on a sunny beach by the sea as starve in a smoky city with factory chimneys belching out pollution. It's much healthier. I often wonder why the unemployed of our great industrial cities don't migrate to the coast. The fresh air and the sun would bring a little colour to their cheeks, at least, and they could fill in the long idle hours with fishing, boating and swimming, and nice long invigorating walks across the cliffs and so manage to keep themselves reasonably fit for any eventual work that might come their way. But that apart, their unemployment benefit and National Assistance money would go a long way towards helping the out-of-season economy of any coastal town they chose to patronise.

I didn't have a bass drum in Clacton. I'd sold it in Manchester. I didn't get a lot for it, just enough for two bus fares to London. I still had the snare drum, cymbals and the rest of the gear though and when we finally landed a job in a pub I improvised a bass drum out of an old tea chest. There was already a resident pianist working this pub and without encroachment on his position in any way, with his approval actually, we succeeded in chatting the guvnor into allowing us to augment with him into a trio. The guvnor agreed to pay us thirty shillings a week each and granted us leave to take a box round and make a collection among his customers, provided we didn't embarrass or badger them into putting more in the box than they could afford and thereby making his pub too expensive for them to drink in.

'They're poor people,' he said, 'and I don't want you lot nicking their beer money.' They were poor people all right. The first night we collected one and sixpence from a room with thirty people in it. Well, there were some really good-looking girls we knew working at the local Butlin's camp. One of them was my wife Connie – we were just good friends then. (After thirty-five years of marriage we still are. She has occasional attacks of Women's Lib. but nothing serious.) They were real shrewdies with plenty of nous who knew their way about and we got them at it taking the box round and the take shot up immediately. Also, as there were four or five of them, and none of us ever left the stand, all of them were as sharp as tacks, they were able to manoeuvre that box around the pub with the kind of subterfuge and dexterity that was far too devious for the guvnor to keep track of. They worked that box with a finesse that would have put many an old-time busker's bottler to shame. They were filling it twice and three times a night. A lot of it was pennies but we could nearly always change a fiver at the end of the evening, that is if you didn't mind it in copper. One of us would take it to the bank every day and get it changed into larger currency and one day the clerk said to us, 'Where d'you work? Down a public lavatory?'

We were doing very well now, and the word was getting around about us and a lot of jazz fans were coming in to listen. This bar was really jumping now most nights; the pianist was pretty lousy, he was well below our standard, but so long as he kept out of the way, and didn't drag the beat his limitations weren't too obvious to many but us. We were getting a bit worried about all these jazz fans though, they weren't big drinkers and they took up a lot of seating space. Half a pint a night seemed to be just about their capacity which wasn't very good for trade. But there were a lot of girls coming in now and the place was becoming a number one must and the till up at that bar was ringing furiously.

One night an old tramp with a battered violin climbed up on to the stand and sat in with us. It was a bit of a giggle for a while, he was so bad he was funny and amused the crowd for a bit. But come the end of the evening he wanted the box split four ways and we said, 'No.'

'But I played, didn't I?' he said, 'I played.'

'But we didn't want you to play,' we said.

'But I did play, didn't I?' he said, 'Mean, I could have been somewhere else earning, couldn't I? If I hadn't played here.'

'Where d'you normally play?' I said.

'On the beach,' he said.

'Well, stay on the beach,' I said.

'It's no good on the beach,' he said. 'They don't give you no money down there I mean, you can play all day there ... on that bloody beach an' get nothing, nothing at all ... 'cept a lot of abuse. I was told to piss off, I was. Bloody Punch an' Judy man. Told me to piss off he did. I was giving him a bit of accompaniment. A bit of musical accompaniment. Piss off, he said. I said there's scope for two hats here. Piss off, he said. I said they have pianos in the pictures, they used to. Piss off, he said, 'fore I give you one. I said I might give you one mate. I've done a bit. I've done a bit in me time. I can handle meself. Don't worry. Bloody toe rag. It's not his bloody beach. They don't want to watch that bloody Punch an' Judy. Not without a bit of music. A bit of accompaniment. I was here first, I said. I was here last year. He wasn't. So I told him. Piss off, I said. Piss off back where you come from.'

'Ain't you going to give me nothing?' he said.

'No,' I said.

'Not for playing all them songs?' he said. 'Look, some of that's mine. Some of that's been put in for me.' Then he started appealing to the crowd. 'They're trying to do me out of my money,' he said, 'I played with 'em. You saw me. I played as well ... now they won't give me my share.'

'Give him his money,' someone said.

'Come on,' I said to Peter and the pianist, 'let's scarper.' I could sense trouble.

'No you don't,' said the tramp. 'No you don't.'

Then some drunk started to get nasty.

'Give him his fucking money,' he said.

'Fair's fair, he played as well,' a woman said.

''Course he played,' the drunk said.

'Picking on him 'cos he's old,' the woman said.

'T'ain't fair, he played as well.'

'You saw me,' the tramp said to the woman.

'I saw you,' the woman said to the tramp.

'I played as well,' the tramp said.

'Give him his money . . . you fucking cheats,' the drunk said.

By now the guvnor was over.

'Give him his money,' the guvnor said, 'and don't bring him in here any more.'

Reluctantly we gave him a share. The next night he was in again.

'Piss off,' I said.

'I've given up the beach,' he said, 'there's no money down there.'

'Piss off,' Peter said.

'This is the only place you'll pick up a bit of money,' the tramp said. 'They get a few drinks down 'em they get daft an' they give you money.'

'Piss off,' the pianist said.

'I'll do one for fun,' he said. 'Just for fun, I'll do one.'

'Piss off,' said the guvnor. Then he turned to me and said, 'I thought I told you not to bring him in here any more?'

'I didn't bring him in,' I said.

'You encourage him,' the guvnor said.

'I encourage him?' I said.

'You gave him money, didn't you?' the guvnor said. 'You give him money. 'Course he'll come in. What d'you expect? You give him money . . . he's bound to come in.'

'But . . . ' I tried.

'Don't argue,' the guvnor said. 'I don't want him in here stinking the place out. Get rid of him.'

And with that he walked away.

'I'll just play a couple,' said the tramp. 'Just the one. I want to see what you're doing.'

And he started to play what sounded like *Phil The Fluters Ball*. 'It's going all right,' he said. 'They seem to like it.'

He scratched away at his fiddle a bit more, then stopped.

'How was that?' he said. 'What was that?'

'It sounded a bit like *Phil The Fluters Ball*,' said Peter.

'Ah, was that it?' said the tramp. 'Yes, it might have been.'

He scraped away at a few more bars, listening attentively, his head cocked on one side.

'Ah yes,' he said, 'I think it is. You've got it, I think. *Phil The Fluters Ball* you say, I didn't know I knew that. That'll come in handy that will. Here . . . what's this one?'

And he played *Phil The Fluters Ball* again but somehow differently.

'It's *Phil The Fluters Ball*,' said Peter.

'Ah, well, I know that twice then. That'll be handy that will, that'll come in useful. Well, I suppose we'd better start eh? They're ready for a few jigs.' And he sat in with us again.

Peter and I were kipping on a couple of spare beds in the girls' billet at Butlin's, using the staff canteen, and making ourselves pretty much at home there. But this night for some reason we couldn't sleep in the billet. I think, if I remember rightly, a couple of new girls had been taken on, and our beds had been given to them. And so we thought we'd go down on the beach, it was a warm night, and we made ourselves reasonably comfortable in a bus shelter just off the sands and settled down for the night. The bench was a bit hard but we were under cover and out of any rain that might fall and off the sand which I hated sleeping on – well the bloody stuff gets in your hair, your clothes, everywhere, and itches like mad giving you the feeling it's running alive, which it probably is. Well, all those sweaty bodies lying on it all day and the tide didn't bother to wash it. We had just about stopped talking and were beginning to doze off when along the beach loomed this figure with a violin under his arm.

'Here comes Heifetz the wandering minstrel,' said Peter.

And in walked the tramp. He glared at us through his watery eyes and said,

'What are you doing here?'

'Having a kip,' I said.

'Up!' he said. 'Up! Up! Out! It's mine,' he said.

'What are you talking about?' I said. 'This is a bus shelter. How can it be yours?'

'It's mine,' he said, 'I sleep here. Everyone knows that. Everyone knows I sleep here. Ask 'em if you don't believe me.'

'Look, we're sleeping here tonight,' I said. 'We were here first.'

'No, you wasn't,' he said. 'I was here first. I was here before you was born.'

'Look,' I said, 'anyone can sleep here. It's a bus shelter.'

'Not at night,' he said. 'It's not a bus shelter at night. At night, when them bloody buses stop – it's mine; it's where I bloody live. Go an' ask the Council. I look after all this beach for 'em. From here mate right down to Jaywick. To Jaywick Sands an' back. You're dealing with someone when you deal with me. You're not dealing with rubbish. I belong here. I know 'em all. They all know me. But vagrants, mate – vagrants – they don't need 'em. See? If you get my meaning. People. They want people. Spending people. But not vagrants. This beach is all closed at night anyway. It's shut down. They don't want you lot. Walking all over it. Getting it dirty. They want it clean, mate. They want it kept clean. For the people. The people in the morning. They don't want you all over it. Dropping rubbish. Making a mess.'

He pointed at the darkened beach.

'This is for people, mate. All this is for people. It's kept private for people, mate . . . not vagrants. You walk on that, mate . . . you set foot on that and they'll have you. I'll have you. They'll have you. They'll have your footsteps. Your feet prints.'

'Piss off,' said Peter. 'We trying to get to sleep.'

'This ain't a hotel,' the tramp said. 'This ain't a hotel you know. You can't come in here dinging bells an' asking for bloody rooms. Anyway, we're shut. We've all gone home. So piss off! We're not open.'

We simulated heavy snoring, feigning sleep and hoping he would go away. But through slightly open lids I could see him standing there staring at us in silent fury and chewing his lips. Finally he spoke.

'All right,' he said, 'give me five bob an' you can stay. How's that fit? Does that fit you?'

'I want a *Daily Mirror*,' I said, 'and tea and toast at half past seven.'

'*Financial Times* for me,' said Peter.

'All right,' he said, 'I'll see to that. Give us your five bob then. I'll put you up. You can board here with me.'

'Look, if you want people to stay here,' said Peter, 'if you want to make a going concern out of this . . . you ought to install a few bloody comforts. Like a bloody fire or something. It's bleeding cold.'

'Fires,' the tramp said. 'They're not keen on fires. They lock up the deck chairs. They didn't use to. Could have a fire then. Had a big 'un once. All that bloody wall was going. That wall there. The police blamed me. Wasn't my fault. It was the wind. The bloody wind changed. The tide turned and the wind changed. Caught all that bloody wall it did. It was warm though. It was cold too. A cold night last year. I lit a fire with some of the deck chairs. They keep 'em under lock an' key now. That's a new bench that is. That was the fire. It's almost a new shelter. They put me inside 'cos of that. Trying to keep bloody warm. That's all I was doing. Trying to keep bloody warm.'

'Are you Chinese?' I said, I don't know why.

'My mother was . . .'

'Chinese?'

'She let me down. She could have married well . . . but she let me down. She married my father.'

'Was he Chinese?' I said.

'He couldn't stand 'em,' the tramp said. 'One thing he couldn't stand. He couldn't stand foreigners. Anyone who wasn't English. Bloody cow. Bloody cow she was. He didn't mind Indians . . .'

'Your mother?' I said.

'Bloody magistrate. Put me inside she did. Blamed me. Blamed me for the fire she did. I didn't mind though. Not that summer. It was bloody cold. It was one of them bloody cold summers it was. It wasn't warm I tell you that. His brother was Indian. Well, half of him was ... I was glad to get into the nick that summer ... I don't mind telling you ... I don't know what the other half of him was ... it wasn't Chinese though ... he didn't have any colour ... not to speak of ... not that you'd notice.'

'What are you?' Peter said.

'Eh?'

'What make are you?'

'Who me?' the tramp said. 'I'm not foreign. You can't pin that on us. We've always been English. Specially our side of the family. Don't know what me mother's side was ... but they wasn't foreign ... they was different on me father's side ... but they was mostly English ... 'Cept me grandmother ... she wasn't as English as some of the others ... but she wasn't foreign ... Four months that cow give me ... I didn't mind though. I told her, I said to her, I said I don't mind, I told her ... not in this weather. Well, you're better off ain't you? You're better off inside a summer like that ... I always like to get inside if the weather's bad. I like to get into the nick before the hard weather sets in. You're better off. You're better off in the nick during a cold spell. I like to spend Xmas inside. That's the weather for nick that is. See, it's no good being outside when the bad weather sets in. Not when the snow's about. Not when there's frost around. I had to spend Xmas outside one year. It nearly done for me. I done me thing see. I got meself in trouble for the winter. I done that all right. An' the bloody courts was crowded an' they couldn't hear me case. I thought to meself I thought by the time they get to hear my case it'll be bloody summer. So I went across to the prison see. I went across to 'em an' knocked on the door an' asked for the guvnor. Can I come in I said. Piss off, he said. Yer case ain't been tried yet he said, so piss off. That's all very well, I said, but I'll freeze out here. I want to be in for the holidays, I said. I want to be in for me

Southend ... where the élite meet to eat.

Hop picking ... we had earwigs too here. A boy said to me: 'I've got forty earwigs and fifty bugs in this matchbox.' 'Blimey, they're a bit crowded,' I said. 'Sod 'em!' he said. He grew up to be a landlord.

RIGHT: Me fighting Hitler – if only Monty had known I was there!

OPPOSITE: Frankie Howerd ... making our script sound funny.

Drummer's eye view.

TOP LEFT: Michael Caine in *The Compartment*.

BELOW LEFT: 'It's a good set I know, Johnny – but you've gotta think of something funny for us to do!'

TOP RIGHT: Dennis Main-Wilson, who Sammy Davis re-named, Dame May Whitty.

BELOW RIGHT: 'With a bit of luck, it won't grow up to look a bit like him.'

ABOVE: Alf down under. 'Bloody flies! It's not a white man's country!'

ABOVE LEFT: *All in the Family*. I thought I might have made some money out of that!

LEFT: Deep in thought? Or perhaps it's a tax demand?

Well ... and yet some people would prefer Paul Newman!

pudding an' me turkey ... All me cards are in there, I said. You got all my Xmas cards in there, I said ...'

He droned on like this through a night of broken sleep and scattered dreams.

'I saw that war coming before Chamberlain ... I knew Hitler ... I knew what he was up to ... He didn't fox me ... They wasn't Jews he was burning ... He was one himself ... They was all Jews ... Goebbels ... Himmler ... He was a paper-hanger ... that's how he started ... hanging paper ... decorator ... that's what he was ... painter an' decorator ... that's how he started ... before he got on ... interiors he done ... he done the outsides as well ... but insides mostly ... mostly interiors ... 'Course Churchill was a painter ... he was in that game ... he could use a brush too. Don't know about Chamberlain ... but Winston had a trade ... he was skilled. He was skilled same as Hitler ... He done up Downing Street. He done all that up ... Repointed the roof ... he was handy with a trowel ... that's where he was handy ... with a trowel ... he was skilled. I've always been skilled. One of my strong points that is ... always has been. You got to have skills ... you couldn't live out of doors ... not without skills ... not like I do ... not without skills ... not my age ... most my age is sitting about moaning on pensions. Been round the world I have. Twice. If not three times. See ... get a job in the docks see ... that's how you do it ... take any rubbish they will down there ... they ain't fussy. Get yourself fixed up in the docks ... an' smuggle aboard ... an' hide ... keep yourself hidden till four miles out ... show yer face then ... need to show yer face then for eating. An' he ain't going to turn back just to put yer off ... an' inconvenience all them what's paid ... an' throw his charts out ... I mean ... they put you to work but ... but I've had people try to put me to work before ... better people than them ... but they're all busy see. He's got a big boat to drive ... an' a lot of bloody customers to look after an' all that. He can't chuck you over the side ... that's murder ... murder on the high seas ... an' the captain see ... he don't want to get his self topped do he? Eh?'

Then he laughed for a long time, ending in a mirthless dry clucking that sounded a bit like the last rattles. It was a terrible night with my back aching from the hard bench, and the continual flitting in and out of shadowy nightmares, with this nickering bray and a convulsive sea. They say that the waves of a sea come in sevens, six small ones preceding a big one. Well, that night the rhythm of the waves was all over the place. They didn't know where they were. They had the kind of beat our wandering Heifetz had.

We gave him five bob in the morning. We didn't give it to him out of sympathy or any other charitable motives. We gave it to him because we knew it was either that, or having to throw stones at him to make him go away.

We didn't have to bum around the beach at night for long, nor in the day time, which we didn't mind, lying flat out on our backs when it was sunny or mooning about in cafés drinking gallons of tea when it wasn't, which was more often the case. We all got a job in a small guest house – Peter, Connie, a friend of hers, Ivy, and myself. We were still playing in the pub at night but during the day I was head cook and bottle washer in this guest house; Peter was my assistant and both Connie and Ivy were chambermaids. We had things very much our own way in this guest house, the people who owned it couldn't find anyone to work in it, they could hardly find anyone to stay in it either. The food under my culinary regime was good, wholesome and reasonably cooked – if you ate in the kitchen with the staff. What was served in the dining room was another matter. My wife is a vegetarian and in those days if you were a vegetarian, Christ, you had no chance. If you told them you didn't eat meat they offered you bacon or fish. I don't think it's a lot better today in most restaurants. But this guest house, when I was running the kitchen, was a vegetarian's dream. Every meal except breakfast was a salad. Lettuce and eggs. I ran the kitchen there on army lines, which means it was run purely for the cook's comfort. Everyone's favourite breakfast there was bacon, eggs and porridge (it was quite often served in that order – depending on how long the porridge water took to boil, which in turn depended on what time we got up), most days it was the only breakfast. I gave them kippers one day but Ivy, who was on tables, served them with custard – she thought that was how posh people ate them. The kippers were a mistake. I had just started a stock pot and Peter, unbeknown to me, threw the kippers into it. The next morning everybody complained that their early morning tea tasted of kippers. I couldn't understand why this should be until I discovered that Ivy was making the early morning tea from the boiling stock pot. Ivy, who was near blind, and wouldn't dream of wearing glasses, had mistaken the thin colourless stock for boiling water.

My Army training had got me into the habit of using all left-over porridge as a thickener for any soups I made, which led to guests refusing my porridge disdainfully at breakfast, only to end up eating it at lunchtime. The best way I ever saw porridge made was in an Army field kitchen on a bluff oven. A bluff oven is oblong in shape and about fifteen feet in length, the ovens run along each side of it with hotplates on top, and is fired in the middle along its entire length. The fire being directly beneath the hotplates they naturally get red hot. And this goon who was making the porridge – I must tell you first off that most Army porridge chefs are usually the village idiots of wherever they hail from, was cooking it in a dustbin and was standing on the hotplate to stir it. He was dancing about on the hotplate, his gym shoes smouldering and mingling with the smell of burnt porridge. He was yelping with pain from his scorching feet, and his ankles were getting splashed with hot fat from the trays of bacon frying alongside them. He was covered from head to foot in soot, a not uncommon appearance for an Army cook actually. We were issued with white clothing but any cook who managed to keep them white for too long was viewed with suspicion by the rest – well let's face it, cooking is a dirty job especially in a field kitchen where you have to stoke the fires as well as prepare the food. And you can't be off washing yourself every five minutes. This is what would annoy an Army cook, anyone who would ask why the cook looked so dirty, and if they did they'd be in for a lot of bad food.

The whole regiment suffered. It's interesting to watch nature at work, you know, it was odds on that the fellow making porridge was the thickest man in the regiment, the only thing thicker than him being his porridge. Most of the cookhouse personnel were half-wits with a sprinkling of shrewdies. But then, I suppose, you could say that of the entire regiment, or of life in general. The shrewd ones would lie about in bed shouting orders and abuse at the thick ones doing the work. They were rather like village idiots. You could always tell them out in the town when they were on pass, they were covered with greasy patches, and with bits of bacon hanging on to them still. The Military Police never bothered with them. It was useless to charge them, they were what they were, and if the M. P.s had put them on a charge for walking around scruffily dressed they would have probably got no breakfast the following morning, or a breakfast it wouldn't have been wise to eat. So they turned a blind eye to them. It was either let them walk the streets filthy dirty, or risk food poisoning, or at the very least have them spitting on your food before they served it. Village idiots they may have been but they were a law unto themselves in a lot of ways.

For this reason, I never send back the food in a restaurant. If I don't like it I don't eat it. I never send it back and risk the rage of some neurotic chef de cuisine because I am too aware of the odious things he might do to it. I well remember a duty officer who came into lunch late and the cook in charge had forgotten all about him, and the cook, seeing him only as a bloody nuisance coming in out of the blue like that after everyone else had eaten, retrieved him a lunch from the swill bin. It couldn't do him any harm, it was reasonably fresh and clean still, but I am positive he wouldn't have eaten it with such relish if he'd known where it came from. This is why, as I say, I never send back the food in hotels or restaurants, I just don't eat it and make a point of never eating in that place again.

My wife is, as I have said earlier, a vegetarian and once she has declared herself as such, and a nuisance to the kitchen staff of any hotel we are staying at, I move to another table and make out I am not with her. This way only one of us has to risk suffering a bad stomach. Once, after one day of arguing with the kitchen staff of a five-star hotel, she spent the rest of the week in bed with a doctor in attendance. A wise doctor, he attributed her suffering to being a vegetarian in this particular hotel. Needless to say we have neither of us been back there since, nor any of our friends.

Cooks in general, leaving out a few first-class restaurants that I eat in regularly, are a bad-tempered, ill-bred lot who are forced to work in insufferable heat in insanitary conditions. You may be sitting out front in the lap of luxury but rest assured the cook is most probably having a nervous breakdown at the back. They may keep up an air of coolness, quality and hygiene at the front of the house where you are sitting in your expensive seat, and the waiters may be clean and immaculately groomed, but out back, apart from swatting flies and throwing knives at rats, all hell is breaking loose and tempers are exploding. I sat at the bar in one expensive restaurant in the West End of London and witnessed a row going on between the waiters and the kitchen staff. As the service door opened the noise erupted and the air was blue with their language, dying down to quiet decorum when it closed. Needless to say I didn't eat there that night. All food has to be handled and where the cook's hands have been is a matter of conjecture, all you can hope for is that he hasn't some dread disease.

Dwell for a moment. Cooking is not a good job, and can you believe that any really intelligent person would wish to be a cook and work long hours in the terrible suffocating heat of a kitchen? It can only attract the kind of people who do it, simply because they are not fitted for anything else. You will seldom find a Bernard Shaw or a Bertrand Russell working in a kitchen, at least not from choice. About most things I always think to myself, what type of person would do this kind of work and proceed from there. The best brains in Parliament are not always in the Cabinet which is absolute stupidity when you realise that the people in the Cabinet are at the helm of the country.

Anyway, here was I, ill-mannered and ill-bred, preparing and cooking food for the equally ill-mannered and ill-bred gentlefolk who were forced by circumstances, beyond the control of their fixed incomes, to stay in this badly run guest house. Fixed incomes! Their incomes were far from fixed, they were shrinking yearly. They were on a permanent wage freeze. But you couldn't feel sorry for them, these shabby, faded gentility, they hadn't worked since no one knows when. They were living off their share of the profits gained from exploiting the labours of others less fortunate. Parasites all of them. Willing to do anything to keep body and soul together but work. Well, unfortunately for them, the staff of this small guest house where they whiled away their summers were no keener to work than they. They weren't getting value for their money, but then neither had they given value for it either.

One day the guvnor bought a job lot of chickens. They had probably died of fowl pest, because they were young chickens and he normally bought layers when they died of old age. He never bought chickens killed specially for the table. He prayed for an epidemic of cattle pestilence so he could buy cheap meat. Well, the possibility of any of his guests returning for another visit was so remote that it didn't really matter how he fed them, or what on, providing it was cheap. Anyway, it was not worth him buying good food with the kitchen staff he had. He brought these dodgy chickens in whilst we were having our supper and although I know the gentry like their fowl a bit high, I thought these particular birds were flouting the sanitary laws a little. Peter shouted at him,

'Hoi! Don't bring those in here. We're eating. D'you mind!'

There was a terrible cat that hung about the yard at the back of the kitchen. Satan we called it, because its ears stood up like bloody great horns, I suppose. It was the biggest cat I'd ever seen, and wild, really wild. Satan always seemed to have an entourage of other cats prowling around with him, they weren't his body-guard, the one thing he didn't need was protection. He was king of the cat walk in that area, a kind of feline tribal leader. Perhaps it wasn't an entourage so much as a harem that accompanied him, I don't know. I went out into the yard to chase him off with a broom one day – I didn't like the way he sat and stared at us as though we might be food, it made me uneasy and really scared the girls. I shouted at him and threatened him with the broom but instead of turning tail and scampering off like most cats would have done, he not only stood his ground but moved towards me spitting. Christ, those baleful yellow eyes, and that menacing crouch frightened the shit out of me and I shot back into the kitchen and slammed the door. From then on we contented ourselves with throwing things at him from the kitchen window. Well, Satan and his followers had these chickens.

We used to leave a window unlocked at night for Ivy to get in. She was like a cat herself, always out on the tiles at night. She was a bit of a nympho and went right through the card at Clacton, I think. The only people who didn't have her, I think, were the local clerics, the Chief Constable and the Watch Committee, and Peter and myself. Peter had a big crush on her but Ivy didn't fancy him. I asked her why one day and she told me that she liked Peter very much as a person but she didn't fancy him as a lover. Pressed on this she said he was too ugly and she couldn't stand ugly fellows. To have been the ugliest fellow in Clacton that summer must have been something. I didn't realise that Peter was so ugly. I asked her how she knew he was that ugly. As I have said, she was blind as a bat and could hardly see without glasses which she never wore, and she said she'd had him described to her. I tried to reason with her that if she liked his personality so much (she called him a star turn, a favourite phrase of hers for anything she thought fantastic), and taking into account she could barely see him, what did it matter that he was so ugly? She said it was what people would think.

'Well, I'm good-looking, ain't I?' she said.

'Well?'

'Well, I've been told I am,' she said.

'So?'

'Well, it's true ain't it?' she said. 'Everyone says I am. So why should I go with ugly fellows? I'm not a charity.'

'But looks aren't everything,' I said.

'You don't go with ugly girls, though,' she said, 'even Peter don't go with ugly girls.'

'But I don't like any ugly girls,' I said.

'I don't like any ugly fellows,' she said.

'You like Peter.'

'Not to look at,' she said.

'But you can hardly see him,' I said.

'I can imagine him,' she said.

'Well imagine him good-looking then,' I said.

'That wouldn't be fair,' she said. 'That wouldn't be fair to him. I couldn't do that. I couldn't go with him and imagine he was somebody else, somebody good-looking, just to feel sexy. It'd be cheating and I couldn't cheat on Peter. It'd make me feel rotten. No I couldn't do that.'

'Why not?' I said.

'I like him too much,' she said.

'But he's not that ugly,' I said.

'Cross your heart,' she said.

'Yes,' I said.

'Say it,' she said.

'Gawd! Cross my heart.'

'And hope to die in a cellarful of rats; go on, say it.'

'And hope to die in a cellarful of rats,' I said.

'I don't believe you,' she said.

'Gawd! Look,' I said, 'he's no Tyrone Power ... I give you that. He's not as good-looking as me, all right ... But ...'

'You're not good-looking anyway,' she said.

'How d'you know?' I said.

'Even Connie doesn't think you're good-looking,' she said. 'And she likes you.'

'Oh, piss off,' I said. 'Bloody girls. It's all you think about.'

Anyway, Satan had all these bloody chickens because of her. When we came down in the morning they were just a pile of bones. If the guvnor had caught that bloody cat the guests would have had cat casserole instead of roast chicken that day. For a while I thought he might put Ivy in the pot, he was that mad. Actually I had a soft spot for that cat. He was an outsider and a rebel and he didn't run like most cats do, he stood his ground. I'd have put money on him against any dog.

You know, years ago when I was a kid, there was a big market near where I lived and they used to sport with rats there every Sunday morning. It was one street this market, all shops and stalls, and they used to catch all these rats and cage them until

Sunday. And they'd bring their dogs, good ratting dogs all of them, and line so many cages across the road and bet on how many rats the dogs would kill and how far the last rat would be from its cage before the dog got to it. There was a fellow there one Sunday wanted ten cages up for his dog, ten rats, and was betting big money that the last rat wouldn't get further than five feet from its cage. It was a great little dog, straining at the leash when it saw the rats, it's head and face pocked with scars. Well, when its owner had got enough money on they let all these rats go, all at once simultaneously with the dog. You've never seen anything like it. Christ, this dog was fast. And if my childhood memory serves me right, the last rat, when they measured, wasn't three feet from its cage. Satan would have been great at that.

After their morning's sport they would all adjourn to the adjacent pub and there was a fellow there who would bite a rat's head off for a pound. The way he did it, if you want to try, he'd put a big leather gauntlet on his hand before he reached into the cage for the rat, and he would hold it in such a way that it couldn't turn in his hand or move its head too much. Then, holding the rat upside down with its mouth to the roof of his own mouth so that it couldn't bite his tongue, he'd snap quickly at it, biting hard with all the strength of his jaws. (Don't try it if you wear dentures.) Then he'd spit the rat's head on to the floor and down a pint of beer with a couple of large scotches in it – to disinfect his mouth he used to say. It wasn't vermin he worried about though, it was the rat moving in his hand. If it should twist out of your grip it was down your throat and would make its own way out of your arse.

Our friend Heifetz turned up at the back door of the kitchen one day – his grapevine must have been good – so we put him to washing-up, chopping wood, and fetching coal, etc., for all he could eat. He ended up kipping on the kitchen floor. Well, Peter and I at about this time were getting hooked on Steinbeck and Marx and Engels (this was just before Shaw). Ivy thought they were a chain store. And the tramp was our own tame Steinbeck character. Steinbeck was the first good novelist I'd read. Up until then all I'd read was fiction and all the characters in these books were imaginary and only lived in the minds of their authors, they were stillborn on to the page and their feelings were about as human as the paper they were written on. Steinbeck, on the other hand, was writing about people who lived in the world as I knew it, and not just in his own mind. This kind of writing was a revelation to Peter and me and we went around Clacton discovering Steinbeck characters everywhere. The whole of Clacton was Steinbeck. The tramp was Steinbeck. Ivy was Steinbeck. Some people, like the customers in this awful guest house, weren't Steinbeck because they weren't real.

I found writers of characters like this much more interesting. Well, they were writing about people like myself, people up against this business of trying to live without being exploited too much by the other bastards. Or having to work too hard at doing things you weren't the slightest bit interested in, just for a few bob to keep body and soul together so you could go on doing the same stupid things all over again, like mice on a bloody treadmill, going round and round and round again and not being able to get off the bleeding thing. Some got drunk and fell off it, but they had to climb back again as soon as they sobered up, that is if they want to get drunk again – or eat. The only thing I could do was play my kind of music – jazz. And before I could earn a living doing this I had to find an audience, and there I was really struggling, because guys playing great jazz even couldn't find an audience. I had as much chance of finding an audience for the music I played as I had of growing two heads. What did I want two heads for anyway? I couldn't feed the mouth on the one I already had.

9 Back to 'Straight from the West End'

This was the big problem facing me when I left Clacton. I hadn't thought about writing then. The only writing I did then was to write my name down at the Labour Exchange. This went on for a few years. I invented all kinds of terrible stories why I couldn't work. I had no real reason why I couldn't work – except laziness. And that wasn't a good enough excuse. I think laziness is a very good reason for not working, in fact I can't think of a better one. But you can't reason with people like that. So long as you were able-bodied, fit and healthy, they couldn't see any reason why you shouldn't work. And I didn't have anything wrong with me like T. B. or any other disease I could fall back on. I was healthy and fit for work but I didn't consider the work fit for me. And there lay the trouble. My future as a jazz musician looked pretty black. My future as any kind of musician looked pretty black. I spent a lot of time trying to persuade a lot of publicans of their need for a band like ours but they didn't see it at all, they said it interfered with their customers drinking – when we played the pub emptied. So that market was rapidly shrinking. I got a job in one pub playing with a blind pianist – he didn't pay me much – but it was work. I soon discovered though that all he wanted me for really was to act as a seeing eye dog for him. I used to have to take him to the toilet and he'd piss up my leg. He couldn't point it right and I wasn't going to get hold of it and point it for him. So I used to push him through the door and then get out of his way and let him piss up somebody else's leg. I left him after a while – well my dry cleaning bill was getting to be enormous. He was a lousy pianist anyway.

The real reason actually was that Peter and I were starting to get a better class of work. Peter was a pretty good alto and I was a pretty good drummer. I was above average, anyway. When it came to the Tony Crombies, I didn't compare, except to the unmusical, and there was an awful lot of those about. Some of these even thought I was better than Tony Crombie, and of course I never discouraged that belief. Peter and I were getting jazz dates in places where musicians like Tony Crombie and Ronnie Scott wouldn't go. These dates we were getting were too far from the West End for them. They hardly left Archer Street except to go home at night. One of these dates was at Maidstone but by the time we'd paid our fare there and back we weren't a lot in. But in Maidstone we really meant something. We were from London, straight out of the West End, we always played out of it, we never played in it. In the West End we were just music lovers, but out of the West End we were rated class jazz players. They were all oafs and what they thought about our playing didn't amount to much outside of Maidstone unfortunately. We didn't like Maidstone much anyway, there were too many fields between it and London, and besides I'd been held a prisoner in the nick there before being sent on to Sowerby Bridge. I never felt at home in the country in those days. I'm not all that enamoured by it now if it's too isolated. Poets who rave about it leave me cold. The only use it seems to have is for growing things in. If I read some poet on about a field with ears of corn trembling towards the sun . . . I see work. I see people having to cut it and bundle it on to lorries. A field of corn looks like a lot of hard labour to a layabout like me. Fine Georgian mansions and their lovely gardens and well timbered parks with a Rolls on the front drive have always looked better than fields to me. Especially if I am looking out of one of the windows, or sitting behind the chauffeur in the Rolls.

I'm a natural layabout I suppose and it's my ambition to be a rich one. It's terrible to be a layabout though sometimes, because it isn't all that important to a layabout unless it's made easy. Writing comes reasonably easy to me and when I hear some writers moaning about the agonies they go through with the nerve-racking lonely anguish of creation and the torture of putting words on paper, I think, Christ, they ought to have a go at humping bricks, or toting bales in the docks. Shaw always said that writing came so easy to him that he found it hard to understand why everyone couldn't do it. Well, hard or not, it's a lot easier load than most people carry. Most writers are critics, sitting with their feet up and a fag lit, having a nag, or if they've got a sense of humour, poking fun at all that's going on around them. There's a lot to be said for the layabouts' philosophy, at the very least things are well thought out before you do them. If there were more layabouts in the world and less was done it wouldn't be altogether a bad thing. There'd be far less wars declared or fought and a lot less troubles caused in many ways because it would all be too much bother. 'If I felt a bit more energetic or I wasn't sitting so comfortable, I'd get up and whack him.' Which the good layabout is loath to do. It means getting up, which is what first put me off religion, I suppose. You had to get up on Sundays, put on your best suit and go to it. I could never see the point in climbing out of bed, getting dressed, putting your best suit on and walking up to the church just to sit and listen all over again to roughly the same sermon you heard last week. It wouldn't have been so bad if the vicar had been an entertaining speaker. At least in the theatre you have got a reasonable chance of getting something new once in a while. It isn't like the telly though. That's a marvellous invention right by your chair. You don't have to get involved in too much movement to turn that on. I watch a lot of telly, I suppose, only because once I've turned it on I'm too lazy to get up again and turn it off. I have been thinking about getting one of those remote controls fitted to my armchair, I think if I had one of those I would be a lot more selective in my viewing. I watch a lot of awful rubbish at the moment but I find it very soporific and much more pleasant to take than sleeping pills. It's safer too, no one has died yet from an overdose of telly. I think the reason a lot of shows get their big figures is because people are too lazy to turn them off.

I think the trait of laziness is a good one and we should encourage in our children and really question every task before attempting it. Is it worthwhile doing this? If you're not too sure stay as you are and concentrate. Only move when it's really essential to, like when you want to eat, and only do that when you feel hungry. A lot of people only eat because it's the thing to do, or to keep busy. As soon as some people wake up the first thing they think of is breakfast. They've been lying in bed for hours doing absolutely nothing but as soon as they wake up they've got to be doing something so right away it's breakfast. And then they wonder why they get fat.

I was reading about an old chap in an advanced stage of senile decay and it said he kept falling asleep all day long. Which is not a bad habit for anyone if you've nothing better to do. I wouldn't call that senile. A lot of people do that even when they've got something to do. I knew a fellow who was always falling asleep while having sex with his wife, and as they were always at it he got plenty of rest. This old chap kept falling asleep obviously because he had nothing better to do, I mean, what is there to do when you're in an advanced stage of senile decay? What worried the doctor and all the nurses was every time he woke up he kept asking for his breakfast. The doctor said this was very dangerous to his health because all he was eating were breakfasts and that his diet consisted of porridge and egg and bacon. Of course, all they had to do really was give him soup, roast beef and Yorkshire pudding if it was lunchtime when he woke up. Let him call it breakfast if he wanted to.

So you want to rush about? Well, if it's for yourself you want to rush about, rush about, but don't rush about for other people unless you are getting well paid with a very good pension at the end of it. Even then, try and find something a bit interesting to rush about for. I worked for a time at Briggs Bodies, a subsidiary of Fords. I worked on an assembly line and it was awful. I was tightening nuts on car bodies and every now and again the foreman would come along and speed it up and we'd slow it down again and this went on all day with me and a lot of other people missing out nuts all over the place. This is why on a lot of cars the bodies start to fall to pieces and strange rattles begin to appear after only a few months on the road. We weren't bothered. None of us could afford to buy a car in those days, so as we weren't going to be riding in them when they fell to pieces, we weren't too concerned. We got our wages whether they fell to pieces or not. You see, they paid us such low wages that there wasn't a chance in hell of any of us to own a car so we didn't really care if they worked or not. The moral to this story is, of course, that you should always give people good wages and a pride in their work if you want something worthwhile. Of course, they give car workers very good wages today but the cars still fall to pieces after a few months, if they go at all.

In the old days when this country was full of craftsmen they took a pride in their work and they not only made solid furniture, they carved and inlaid patterns on it. The only pattern you will find on modern furniture is if you scrape the veneer and find a stencil pattern – 'Fyffes Bananas' or 'Open Other End'. They made chairs as pretty as a picture to look at. Now it takes you all your time to get a chair that is comfortable to sit in, let alone look at. These days manufacturers don't so much serve your need for things as create your need for things. A really happy man is a man who has been able to rid himself of all the things he doesn't really need. In an ideal society you wouldn't own a thing you didn't really need. Want is the awful need. To want is a struggle to have and an idiot pursuit. I needed a house and so I got a house. But I wanted a big imposing sort of house and I got one, and now I have to work like a bastard to keep it up. I have never been interested in buying houses as an investment though. Buying them and turning them into overcrowded bed-sit slums for others to live in. I have never been avaricious in that respect, like some greedy piggish squirrel hoarding property and food to sell at inflated prices to others. Even the monkey we look down on only takes his immediate fill from the tree of nuts leaving the rest for the next hungry monkey who comes along. Money should be for spending, to satisfy one's needs only, but then some people's needs are greater than others, the greedy bastards. Money affects people in strange ways, it ruins some. Some people when they gain a lot of money drink themselves to death in a few years, and give it back to the country in death duties. Good citizens these. We should strike a medal for them. He drank for his country's prosperity. Apart from death duties, the tax alone on alcohol and tobacco contribute enormously to the country's wealth and we all know how dangerous it is to drink or smoke in excess, but still a great number of tremendously brave people do it, and should be rewarded for their patriotism. So the next time you see a drunk weaving his way unsteadily across the floor of your local pub, his fingers stained yellow with nicotine, go up to him and shake him by the hand, buy another drink for him or stuff another cigarette in his mouth before he hands you a white feather, because the man's a hero and is drinking and smoking himself to death for Queen and Country.

I know a rich person who stands, with her work-worn fingers covered in diamonds and roughened by soap, breaking her back over a copperful of dirty washing because she is too mean to buy herself a washing machine and spin drier. If she'll treat herself like that, how do you imagine she'll treat her servants or work people?

To me my home is my home and nothing more, if it turns out to have been a shrewd investment then that's all to the good, although, I must say it didn't seem much like an investment while I was struggling to buy it. My wife, Connie, goes around buying old paintings, nothing expensive, she likes them and they go well with the wallpaper, enlivening the walls no end. Some of them may be valuable, I don't really care, they are all worth a bit more than we paid for them. They were painted by artists who, I suppose, were in their way primitive photographers, photographers without a camera. They were men with a flair for painting scenes and people, and they would go around the streets of the East End, or country villages, painting the inhabitants in much the same way as street photographers in more modern times. The people would stand outside their door, or lean against their railings, and this fella would paint you while the kettle boiled, or the dinner was cooking. He would then either flog it to you, providing you liked it, or give it to you for a meal and a pint of beer perhaps. These men painted from door to door and when they weren't painting you they'd paint your knocker, and the more they painted the better some of them became at it. Some of them were very good artists, unsung, and very seldom hung except in the living rooms of those they painted. They probably didn't want to paint you anyway, or your ugly family, but were forced to for the price of a pint and a piece of bread and cheese. For instance, can you imagine Michelangelo thinking to himself, 'I must paint the ceiling of the Sistine Chapel'? I feel sure he would have preferred to paint his work of art on something else rather than lie on his back with paint dripping all over him. The man was a great artist but those idiot Cardinals treated him more like an interior decorator. (Apparently the French looked on Rodin more as a plasterer than a sculptor merely because he hadn't been licensed by the Academy.) I saw lesser artists in the Army painting and decorating some of the stately homes of England with the graffiti of the day, unfortunately they weren't Michelangelos and the stuff had to be washed off or painted over.

Most of those who write on shit-house walls are budding writers, probably of TV comedy, or so some people would like to think. Well, we all have to make a start somewhere and sitting about your natural business, with time on your hands, isn't a bad time to begin. I never use public toilets if I can help it. Well, they're not fussy who they let in to them are they? I always prefer to shit at home in comfort if I can, or at least some place decent. I hate to shit in hovels. I prefer to shit in places like Claridges, or Harrods. If you've got to shit out, at least shit in a place that's got a bit of class. I've shit in better places than some people live in. I remember once, staying in the Royal Suite in the Royal Garden Hotel, and a friend came to visit me there and after using the bog, which was replete with gold fittings, he remarked to me a bit shamefacedly,

'Blimey. It's a bit smart in there ain't it? It don't half make the old prick look shabby.'

I was forced by railway food to use the toilet in the old Euston

105

Station one day and it was horrible. Half of the cubicles were occupied by tramps taking a day off and just like the shit-house at Wembley Stadium, it was ankle deep in piss.

The writing on the walls of the all night shit-house in Leicester Square has to my knowledge been there since time immemorial. They seemed to treat it as if it were some kind of lavatorial National Gallery, nobody ever attempted to clean the walls down there, or wash off the various inscriptions and messages to absent friends. I was in the one at Leicester Square one Christmas Eve and on the wall some joker had written, 'We wish all our readers a Merry Xmas'. I think some people used the Leicester Square toilet as a forwarding address, because I saw the attendant write on the back of a letter, 'Unknown at this address – try Tottenham Court Road.'

One curious aspect of the show business world which I have always thought ironic, and dates back I suppose to the days when thespians were regarded as little more than vagabonds, is the terribly drab and uncomfortable dressing rooms that major stars have to live in when playing theatre dates. A star may have his name spelt in three foot high neon capitals over the front of the theatre and be taking home a fortune in wages, but his dressing room in most cases will be little more than an airless slum. He lives at home probably in a beautiful architectured house amid acres of landscaped greenery and all the other elegant trappings of success but when he works in the theatre he has to leave all this affluence and spend most of his time in a scruffy hovel of a dressing room and most likely shares one or two badly plumbed toilets with the rest of the cast. You see, the theatre is similar to the restaurant, all the magic is out front. Although back stage of a theatre, despite the dreadful living conditions, has its own peculiar magic. It's where dreams come true. But it's also a place where egos can get bruised or savagely battered. I imagine the reason the stage door area is badly lit is because in the old days the people who tended to congregate around stage doors were mostly debt collectors and unmarried mothers looking for the smooth chatting Jack, the lad who'd dropped them in it.

10 Honest employment at last

During one period of financial crisis and with my own small band of debtors pressing me hard (not many would lend me money – this was no reflection on my honesty – it was my obvious inability to pay them back that made them wary) I got a job as a milkman. The work couldn't be too harassing I thought as most milkmen look quite relaxed and happy characters. It was probably Fats Waller's infectiously happy singing of *My Very Good Friend the Milkman* that caused me to think this way, plus the fact that I had never seen a milkman at work on a cold wet and windy day, because on that kind of day I was usually in bed, or at least indoors, where any sensible person would be with no urgent reason to be up and out. But weather apart, inclement or otherwise, the streets were always well aired before I took to them. So, I suppose, the only milkmen I had ever seen were milkmen at the end of their day; the milkman strolling back to the depot at the head of his electric float, all work done, and looking forward to an afternoon of leisure. I knew about the afternoons off, they were the big attraction, a job that involved work in the mornings only was getting very near to my ideal, but what I was not aware of as yet was the early morning start. I had to be up before the crack of dawn, even the birds weren't up before I trundled my electric trolley out of the yard. And what was even more depressing, the milk-round they gave me was on a large estate of tall buildings and they were all walk-ups, with no lifts, and ten floors to a block. I could see right away that I was going to have to earn my afternoons of leisure, and spend them most likely knackered flat on my back and fit for nothing, if I humped all those crates of milk up all those bloody floors. And it wasn't just that, I mean, you'd deliver their bloody milk and then you'd get all the way down to the bottom again before some silly cow would change her mind and yell down to you for another half a pint or a couple of eggs. Well, they didn't get their extra milk or their eggs, a lot of them didn't even get their regular milk because they were too high up. But the milk company did get a lot of complaints and these mounted daily. It was pretty obvious that I wasn't going to last long in this job. Incompatibility was building daily between me and the milk company, who weren't prepared to employ a milkman who wasn't keen to serve customers living any higher than the second floor. I could see their point, they had a contract to supply everyone in these buildings and not just those on the lower floors. So I thought to myself, if I'm going to be sacked for not delivering above the second floor, there isn't much to be gained by continuing my deliveries to the lower floors because any amount of willingness shown here wasn't going to prevent my eventual dismissal; so, resourceful to the last, I dumped the milk in the hallway of each block and let them help themselves. Strangely enough this appeared to be a very satisfactory solution because for a whole week there were no further complaints to the company, or to me, I finished work an hour after starting, and my days, apart from this one hour which was all go, were now lazy and relaxed the way I liked them. I could have gone on like this for a long time. All I had to do was cut that hour down a bit, and start it later, and everything was beautiful. But come Saturday, the day they paid me for their milk, the flipping fly flew in the ointment and got itself really stuck. Nobody would own to having had any milk. Every door I knocked at I got the same answer,

'No mate. Not us mate. We had no milk delivered at all last week.'

'But I left it downstairs in the hallway,' I said.

'Did you?' they said. 'Daft place to leave it. Anyone could take it down there.'

'Someone's had it,' I said.

'Don't doubt it,' they said. 'You leave milk about ... course someone's going to have it. What d'you expect? We ain't had it. No good knocking here.'

I not only got the sack that week-end, I almost got prosecuted for the loss of all that milk.

I had no more success as a baker's roundsman.

Another job I took under pressure and with no intentions of working too hard at. They gave me one of those tall, two-wheeled barrows, and expected me to get between the shafts and pull it around like a horse. It was winter and cold murderous work. My hands got frozen and brought tears to my eyes pulling that cart. There were no tall buildings on my round, but I had two bloody great hills to get up and what they were paying for this wouldn't have fed a horse. It wouldn't have fed me if I hadn't been subsidised by my father. It certainly wouldn't have provided shelter, not even stabling and a piece of dry straw. It's hardly a boost to the ego to know that your only value to an employer is that you're cheaper than a horse. My old man used to say that monkeys were too bloody clever to talk. He always said that if monkeys talked they'd have them working like us. I used to ponder on this a bit when I was a kid, wondering if there was anything to be gained from monkeys. I always cocked deaf-uns when there were any chores to be done about the house in the hope that my mother, weary of talking to a seeming deaf mute, would take the easy way out and ask someone else. At every halt on this baker's round I warmed my hands on the hot bread. It wasn't hygienic I suppose, my hands were always filthy dirty from handling money. It's a funny thing but the bread seemed to make them dirty too, although to be truthful they weren't all that clean when I started. The barrow wasn't all that clean either, it was supposed to be scrubbed every night but nobody ever did it. I did it once and nearly everyone complained of soapy bread so I didn't bother anymore.

Anyway, I still thought there must be easier ways of earning money so I handed in my barrow, went back to the Labour Exchange and told them that I knew the horse was on the way out but I didn't intend to replace him. I said I'd have been better off being a monkey. What they were paying me would hardly have bought a handful of nuts anyway.

The Labour Exchange in those days was like a social club to the fully unemployed who had adapted their way of life to getting by on the dole. We used it as a kind of extension of the local pool room. We hung about there all morning playing cards and bantering with the staff, moving on in the afternoon to the reading room of the Public Library, or one or other of the local cafés. The dialogue down there was as good as you'd get anywhere in that part of London. It was spiced with anecdote and enthralling stories of sexual conquest. I don't think sex before marriage is much of a problem, and it wasn't then, except to those who couldn't get it. I think sex after marriage is the real problem, and to hear them talk a lot of these lads were helping to solve it and keeping a lot of housewives happy and content. Well, it isn't always possible for a chap to feel randy at precisely the same time as his wife does, especially after a hard day's work. And I imagine that the last thing the average working chap wants is to perform an athlete's job on top of his wife after a weary day's slog. And so the lads were giving a hand and probably helped save many a marriage. There may not have been much pornography about in those days but there was a lot of sex. It's a fact, I believe, that those preoccupied with pornography are usually not getting much sex. For instance, dogs don't go in for pornography. You will see them watching a couple at it, but they are only waiting their turn.

One day down the Labour Exchange this joker got his cock out, slapped it on the counter in front of the clerk and said,

'Got any work for this?'

Oh, they were witty.

'Got any work here for a brain surgeon?' another feller said.

'Don't be daft,' said a feller with pimples, lousy teeth and halitosis, 'they ain't got no brains round here.'

'Hey, can't you find him a job?' the first feller said. 'He's stinking the place out. What is that you're wearing? Shit No. 5?'

They all laughed, insensitive to his feelings.

'His mother must have been frightened by a polecat,' someone said.

'I can't help it,' he said. 'I've seen doctors about it.'

'Doctors?' someone said. 'No good seeing doctors, you wanna see a Sanitary Inspector.'

'Stand out of the wind ... you're blowing my way.'

He moved off out of the building. His attempts at fraternization always ended like this. He was a real loner. He had to be smelling like that. No one bothered to find out whether he was a decent bloke or not.

One of the chaps walked in barefoot and wearing just a pair of bib overalls. His old lady had pawned all his clothes while he slept, his boots, everything.

'You don't see trees dashing about all over the place,' an old chap said. 'They stay right where they are.'

'Well, you don't move very often yourself,' said the chap in the overalls.

'See that oak,' he said, pointing out of the window. 'That's been there since I was a boy.'

'You been coming here since a boy? You'll be due for a gold watch soon.'

'What I'm saying,' said the old boy, 'they're livestock ain't they? They're forms of life. I mean, take yer carrot ... yer cabbage ... they're the same.'

'What, same as a tree?'

'Same sort of thing. I mean, yer cabbage is plant life, like yer oak.'

'Gawd blimey ... send him for a cabbage an he'll come back with a fucking tree.'

'Yer oak is like you ... a bloody layabout. Take all the food ... don't move ... don't even care if its acorns grow or not ...'

He'd come across a bit of evolution in the local library.

'He's not being kind-hearted ... an' putting his acorns down for the squirrels ...'

'There ain't no bloody squirrels round here.'

'As soon as one of them acorns starts to grow near him . . . it finds all its food is gone . . . even grass ain't got no chance with trees. It's like yer germ . . . yer microbe . . . he's the same. He's not concerned with you mate. Ain't personal . . . ain't nothing against you personal . . . he ain't picked you out personal to give his disease to . . .'

'Not like that bleeding ginger thing I picked up in Ilford last week. She wasn't too fussy who she give her disease to neither . . . dirty cow! I mean, you go all the way to Ilford where it's a bit more select . . . I mean, you expect it to be a bit cleaner there . . .'

'D'you shop her?'

'I don't know her bleeding name do I?'

'Got to lay off now have yer?'

'No fear. They gave it to me mate . . . bleeding women . . . they can bleeding have it back. Dirty cows!'

'You don't expect that sort of thing in Ilford do yer?'

''Course you don't. Suppose to be posh there . . . all furcoat an' football boots an' they're poxed up to the fucking eyebrows.'

'You ought to be laughing with that.'

'Why?'

'Well, you'll get a bit of sick pay for it won't yer?'

'See . . . with yer germ . . .'

'Shut up about yer fucking germs will yer? I got enough of me own. They've moved into my prick like it was a fucking hotel.'

'I've never had that,' said the feller with halitosis, drifting back into the circle. 'I've never had V. D.'

'Never had a fucking bird that's why. They'd have to wear a gas mask to fuck with you!'

This is how I got my sex education. My first knowledge of sex was gained haphazardly from slovenly old mother nature, and the limited curriculum of the school playground, to be broadened later in Army barracks rooms and the Labour Exchange. For years I fearfully imagined that dread diseases could be contracted merely by putting on a woman's glove or sitting on a lavatory seat. I was brought up in a Roman Catholic household where sex was treated as a dirty thing to be practised only after marriage and with a prayer on the lips beseeching the Holy Virgin to intercede with the Almighty on behalf of the poor sinner who knew no other way of raising a family except by committing a grievous sin. Even a wet dream was punishable and carried the penalty of a string of Our Fathers, and quite often, depending on the whim of some ignorant parish priest, an equal number of Hail Marys. The Roman Catholic Church is built on fear and its prayers and hosannas debased by being inflicted as punishments. You know, the Lord's Prayer is not a bad collection of words – but when it's used like Shakespeare as a bloody big stick it's a bit off-putting.

My mother was a very devout woman and never swore at all, although she had plenty of provocation, and shut her ears to the sounds of the street which to her must have seemed as filthy and unhealthy as the air we were breathing. They never bothered me nor, I think, my father, although he never used them, at least not in our hearing, because I was soon made aware that there were worse things to be encountered in life than bad language. Like the poverty, the awful slum conditions and the dull, degrading exist-ence that would have made even God swear if He had been forced to live in Canning Town with us. They say He's everywhere and Alf Garnett even thinks He goes to West Ham every home game (well, he always said the Prince of Wales did), but I never saw Him down our street or any evidence that He knew it existed and in those days it was only a fourpenny bus-ride from Westminster Cathedral, so He could have popped in if He was interested.

Our parish priest in those days, Father Heenan, didn't let the fourpenny bus fare put him off, he came and lived among us. I don't know whether it was living among us, or whether he was just naturally clever in his own right, but he got himself promoted to Cardinal and posted to Westminster Cathedral. We didn't see a lot of him after that, but I don't think it was the fourpenny bus ride that put him off coming back to see us. I met him years later after *Till Death Us Do Part* was a big success, and he said to me,

'You've done well for yourself young Johnny.'

'You ain't done so bad yourself,' I said.

He was a fan of the show. (Well, he was an intelligent man, and knew all the Alfs, as he'd had to live among them as a parish priest all those years, and he knew Alf was no invention of mine. I've always said I didn't create Alf Garnett, he was created by society; I just grassed on him.) Some years after, when he was Cardinal Heenan, he was introduced to my mother by some Lady something or other, and she said to him,

'This is Mrs Speight, the mother of that brilliant young man who writes *Till Death Us Do Part*. (I'm not putting words in her mouth.) He said,

'I know Mrs Speight very well, we're old friends from the past, I also know her brilliant son and like his work very much.' (I'm not putting words in his mouth either.) He then turned to my mother and said,

'You must be very proud of him?' which totally confused my mother, because she didn't like the show. (Alf's language again. The trouble he gets me into. I must write about people who are more articulate or, at least, don't speak language that gets a yellow card.) To hear this Lady something or other and no less than Cardinal Heenan praising it was completely muddling to my mother. I think she agreed with some other of my many detractors who thought the show should be taken off the air and some dire punishment meted out to me. For her to hear these prominent members of the Catholic hierarchy endorsing this wicked show was to her ears nothing short of Satanic. She expected them all to be struck down without further ado. I'm sure she thought the Cardinal and the Lady had gone bent on her and the Church. My mother enjoyed *The Arthur Haynes Show* but that was a more conventional show, I suppose. Her comment on *Till Death* ... was, so I was told, 'He's gone and spoilt himself.'

My father enjoyed *Till Death* ... better, he enjoyed the local celebrity he got, the praise of his friends. Well, he lived a different life to my mother, he went out to work. But he didn't watch the programme at first. I remember calling round there one day and he was sitting watching ITV, he very seldom watched the Beeb. After a few minutes he said to me, 'I hear you've got a good show on the other side?' I said, 'Don't you watch it?' He said, 'We never watch that side, do we?' It was almost like a religion with him.

ITV was his side, the Beeb was always the other side. At this time the show was at the height of its popularity, the newspapers were full of it, it was headlines some days, and it was clearing the streets at the time it was on.

I was hurrying from the BBC one night to be home in time for the show and the streets were almost empty. Almost home, I thought, what am I rushing for, I've seen it, so I called into my local pub. The bar was empty. I called out,

'Shop! Service!' The guvnor came out and said,

'What d'you want? We're trying to watch your show in there.' And in Australia during those days Warren Mitchell once saw a placard outside a Sydney fish shop which read, 'HURRY UP AND GET YOUR FISH AND CHIPS: ALF'S ON AT EIGHT!' Anyway, that was the situation. Everybody it seemed was watching my show except my father. He only knew about it because his mates at work told him.

11 Back to dishonest employment

About 1952 I got a job collecting insurance. It was a job that had always appealed to me because it seemed easy kind of work, but for years I suffered under the misapprehension that you would have to have degrees or some other kind of qualification to get a job that easy. But it seemed all you need was perseverance and good strong pockets to put the money in. I had never minded handling money. I loved the touch and the feel of it and always dreamt of the day when I might have some of my own; with this job though I could at least strike up an acquaintance with it. The hours were good because there weren't many of them. I only worked Saturdays but had to go out on Mondays to catch those who had given me the slip on Saturdays. Tuesday was spent in laying plans for trapping those who had still managed to evade my net. Wednesday was spent making up my book and paying it in. Thursday and Friday were now devoted to my efforts at writing. I had sold my drums and bought a typewriter with two keys missing. I soon discovered that if you had an inventive turn of mind and could chat and weren't too honest, and allowed the imagination to gallop off on a loose rein, insurance wasn't too hard to sell. They were buying dreams – my dreams.

There's one thing you cannot do and that is to sell insurance honestly. Selling insurance is like selling the clear blue sky. It's an idea and the idea is to get them signed up under any pretext possible. Most people have no wish to buy insurance and to sell it you have to stress the mishaps and misfortunes that could befall them and their kin, and create the impression that not only is it necessary and essential to their future welfare, but that you are giving it to them for almost next to nothing – just a few bob out of good nature and the sense of social responsibility of the company you work for.

If they opened the door and I said, 'I'm selling insurance,' it would be 'Piss off' and the door shut in my face. So when they opened the door I would say, 'I have called about the Family Security Plan,' and they'd say, 'What's that?' and I'd say, 'Haven't you heard about it? Haven't next door told you?' And when they said, 'No,' (how could they have told them – I hadn't called there yet – they were next on my list), I would say, 'Christ, you've got terrible neighbours – I don't know and they talk about Christianity . . . Well, look if I can come in a minute I'll put you in the picture.' And then I'd say, looking round the room approvingly, 'Nice house you've got here.' And they'd say, 'Do you like it?' and I'd say, 'It's a palace – amazing what you can do with these houses if you try – lovely furniture. Now, do you happen to belong to an insurance company?' And when they said, 'Yes, (if they said, 'No,' I explained to them how the Plan didn't work without them belonging and helped them to put it right), I asked them if I could see their book (we were dealing with weekly industrial insurance) and examined the extent of their present cover which I promptly sold back to them with the addition of another two shillings because half of them didn't know what they were insured for or against and the benefits due. And I would go into my spiel thus . . .

'Well, I don't know how I'm going to work this for you but I think you're entitled to it. You see, what's happened – a lot of Insurance companies have suddenly found a lot of money and they are faced with the problem of what to do with it. Now, they can take it to the bank and declare it – but if they do that the tax man is going to take it all – or, and this is why I'm here, they can give it back to you, the people it belongs to.

'Now, as you're a member already you're entitled to some of it but the thing is – how am I going to do it? Was your husband in the War?' (Of course he was – he'd have had to be shrewder than me to get out of that.) 'Yes,' she would say.

'Right – that's it then – you're getting it. First of all, can you afford four shillings a week? It's not that we wish to take this money off you – as I have said, we have a surplus of our own – it's more a kind of stake.'

She would say most probably,

'Oh! Like the Pools you mean?'

And I would say,

'Yes, but better, with us your winnings are guaranteed. The reason you're being asked to pay this four bob is nothing to do with us at all – it's the Government – to show good faith. It's to sort the wheat from the chaff, because as you probably know, without me having to tell you, there are some down this street who aren't worth the four bob – who are, well, least said soonest mended, but you know what I mean. To be honest we'd rather do without them – we'd rather not have them in the scheme at all. Just sign here – and now, if anything happens – get in touch with us.'

And I would then expand on all the benefits that they were already insured for and had been paying for for years, and which she fondly imagined she was getting all over again for this extra four bob. It sounded a good buy and would have been had it been true.

I had no conscience about this because I was just about as poor as they were (actually they were making me richer and letting me get in front a bit) and knew that if I didn't take their money someone else would; some tally man or some other hustler four doors behind me. It was a question of get in quick for what was going before they spent it.

To drum up business and keep them sweet I used to hold these regular burn-ups. There'd be some tatty old carpet in the house of one of my regulars, or an old bedspread, or an old mattress, or a pair of decrepit curtains and I would say to her,

'You've not claimed off us for a while have you?'

And I'd look at this threadbare old carpet and I'd say to her, trying hard not to make it too insulting,

'That's no good, is it? I mean it's a bit old isn't it? How much did you pay for it?'

And she'd say,

'Oh, I don't know. About £10 I think ... it's been a good carpet.'

And I'd say,

'Well, what we're going to do now ... is get you some money.'

And I would light a cigarette and with the match set fire to the carpet, and tell her to put in a claim. Then I would see the local assessor and I'd say to him,

'There's a woman going to claim for a carpet – see she's all right.'

Then I'd make sure that the episode was broadcast as widely as possible, and with the ensuing publicity I'd sign up all the waverers.

Worse than me were the tallymen. They were the real sharks. The way they worked – they'd get this harassed housewife and flog her twelve pounds worth of goods to be paid for (they called it easy terms – they were the hardest I ever saw) over sixteen weeks at a pound a week. After six weeks, not being very bright and a slovenly housekeeper, she will have dropped behind, and her friend the tallyman would say to her over a cup of tea,

'Now let's see if I can sort you out ... '

And he would lend her £12, deduct her debts leaving her the rest to spend how she wanted and to repay him a pound a week over another sixteen week period, and then say to her chaffingly, 'I don't know what you'd do without me sometimes.' I know what she could do without him, and he knew what she could do without him – she could get richer.

Some of these women were really gullible, believing that honesty was the best policy, and were easy pickings for these grasping charmers.

Of course there were a few just as immoral as the tallyman (I was going to say amoral but that means without morals altogether, whereas these had morals – bloody awful morals and deserved each other) and who were taking all they had to offer with no intention of paying and every intention of flogging it which they promptly did before he was hardly out of the street. It was almost a question of in the front door and out of the back before his persuasive sales talk had dried in the air. It was useless suing them because they always promised to pay after pleading poverty, unemployment, chronic illnesses of all sorts. The magistrate would say,

'Can you manage a shilling a week?'

'Yes, your Honour.'

And they would for a week.

The tallymen would quite often stop me and ask me who the good payers were in the street. They wanted me to pinpoint the honest fools – honest folk that would go short rather than have a debt hang over their heads. Nice, easy-to-bleed people, people who flocked to the Colours and faced bombs, bullets and the hardships and sufferings of two world wars to be fobbed off with £8 a week when they became old and fragile and in need themselves. After the big barons of industry and government had stolen their butter, the tallyman came in and nicked their bread. They would come up to me and say,

'What are they like down this street?'

I'd say to them,

'No. 9 – No. 14 – marvellous they are' giving them the two worst payers in the street – families that stole each other's bootlaces and would melt down their mother's gold fillings.

One such family had me chasing about for their money. She was always in arrears and would pay four weeks and miss eight. I got fed up with knocking on the door and hear her call out to her daughter, 'Who is it?'

'The insurance man.'

'Well tell him I'm out.'

'Mum says she's out.'

'When will she be back?'

'He said, "when will you be back Mum?"'

'Tell him to come next week.'

Me: 'You said that last week!'

Mum: 'Where was I then?'

Me: 'Where you are now – hiding in the bloody kitchen.'

With that she'd come to the door saying, 'I must have missed you – I ain't got it now anyway.'

I decided to write her off and stop calling but after a few weeks she button-holed me in the street and said,

'What about my insurance? You've missed me the last few weeks.'

I said, 'I've been missing you ever since I started collecting this book.' She said, 'Well I want my insurance, I don't want it to run out.'

'Look,' I said, 'what insurance? You're not dealing with tally-men when you're dealing with insurance companies. You don't pay and you go out of benefit – and as far as I can see you've been out of benefit for about the last six years – and when you do pay you don't pay enough to get back in. And if I wanted to – if I was dishonest – I could stick to your money you pay me, when you do pay me, because if anything happened then you've got no claim anyway – and if you really want this insurance you'd be better off starting again from scratch. It would be cheaper than paying up what you owe. Think about it,' I said, 'and let us know what you want to do.'

The following week I was down the street collecting when her husband came out. A huge feller he was. He shouted out, 'Oi! I want you. Come here!' I thought Oh Christ. He took me in his house and poured me out a Scotch, 'Good stuff this,' he said. 'For export only – come out of the docks! You're all right,' he said. 'The missus told me what you said and I told her she's taking out that insurance and she's going to pay it regular, every week. It's for her, it's on my life and I've told her, if I catch her in that pub with her gin and stout and she ain't paid you – she'll have a claim off her accident insurance – the silly cow!'

From then on I was able to collect her money monthly, two-monthly, three-monthly, or whenever I wanted – it was safe as if it were in the Bank of England. I marked their card where I could and by levelling with them, they levelled with me, and very soon I had the biggest book in the area and put in less hours collecting it than anyone else in the company.

All this time I was endeavouring to write working class plays about the evils of capitalism and the rights of man, and on the side conning them for a bit of insurance.

I'd got to the end of the jazz road – that hill had been getting steeper the further I climbed.

I think if I hadn't made it as a writer I'd have been one of the top insurance men in the country by now and most likely a lot richer than I am. But I wouldn't have felt so happy because I found that when put to the test an unfortunate handicap of conscience got in the way of my making money. It was a drag I suppose – but there you are.

12 And on to 'Better than being a Jew'

I was introduced to Frankie Howerd by a friend from the Army, backstage at the Prince of Wales Theatre in 1955. He saw some of my work and he showed it to his writers who at that time were Spike Milligan, Eric Sykes, Ray Galton and Alan Simpson. They asked to meet me.

They had an office over a greengrocer's shop in Shepherd's Bush, off the market. I imagined a smart office, all chrome, lush secretaries and Jewish gold watches – instead it was a slum above a greengrocer's.

The first person I met in there was Ray Galton who for some strange reason walks like a queer – he isn't – he's very heterosexual – but he could have fooled me and he did that day. He was wearing seventies'-style clothes in 1955, so you can imagine what he looked like. And to make matters worse Alan Simpson was wearing a red corduroy jacket and seemed to be overfriendly (he is always friendly but I didn't know at the time) and I thought to myself, 'Hello, what's he after?'

I knew a lot of theatricals were bent – Terry Stamp told me that when he became an actor his father said, 'Turned queer then have you?' – so I kept one eye on the way out thinking – 'If any of them start, queers are not too brave – give them a quick kick and head for the stairs shouting, "Help"!'

In those days their manager, Beryl Vertue, always used to be arguing with the greengrocer downstairs about his fruit display, asking him if he could make it less obvious as a lot of important people were coming from the BBC to talk to her clients – this motley crowd that lived upstairs.

The greengrocer wasn't very impressed. I imagine he thought that anybody coming to see that lot wasn't worth moving his fruit for. I always thought Milligan was a bit mad – the greengrocer downstairs was certain he was. I don't think he was any madder than the rest, because here they were, this bunch of near-illiterates, setting out to be writers above a greengrocer's shop.

In those early days I often wondered if I'd chosen right, and if there wasn't more chance of making money downstairs because the way he sold it, it looked like fruit was here to stay. That was in the good old days when fruit was within the average person's price range.

Four doors further down the road there was Smart & Westons, a kind of poor man's Cecil Gee, and where, as soon as I started earning money, I bought my suits. Suits that I fondly imagined were show business suits and made me stand out from the rest, a cut above. I imagined people saying, 'Look at that fellow there – the one with the Smart & Weston suit on – he's someone! Look – him – the hip character talking to Spike Milligan and Eric Sykes!' (Later I found out that no one in Shepherd's Bush knew who they were either.)

Then one day Ray Galton told me what he paid for his suits. 'Sixty pounds?' I said, 'What's it made of?' Right away I saw my suit as others saw it – a cheap suit. I've always had this thing about clothes. If you don't look much yourself, at least your clothes can. Sensible people say that you can only wear one suit at a time, but if you've got 200 suits in your wardrobe at least you've got a change of clothes.

Me and Connie used to go to the recordings to see how it was done. We stopped going after a while because the rounds of drinks in the pub afterwards were so big and I couldn't afford to buy one. It's not so much that I've got any big hangups about being a scrounger, it's just that I didn't want people to notice it –

especially people that you hoped to benefit from in some way. I thought, 'You've got this far, now don't spoil it for a round of drinks'. (Actually they weren't thinking this way at all – it was all in *my* mean, grasping little mind.)

One night I had a count-up between Connie and myself, and pooled our resources so I could get flash and return their hospitality. So I went to the bar and said casually in a voice that I imagined carried all the nuances of ultra-sophistication and all that *savoir faire* crap, 'What are you having fellers?'

Eric Sykes said, 'No, you're our guests this evening,' and brought out a bundle of white fivers as thick as a double-decker sandwich. He pulled one off and threw it on the bar. I looked at it floating in a puddle of beer and thought, 'That's showbusiness – it's even better than being a Jew.'

When I was young it was one of my ambitions to be a Jew. Mosley's Blackshirts were about at the time, going on something awful about the Jews they were, and I couldn't figure it out because every Jew I'd ever met looked a lot better than they did. They were always better dressed, with diamonds on their fingers, and rolls of white fivers in their pockets, and my old man always saying,

'You never see a Jew take his coat off to do a job' – which was the kind of work I was looking for – and I said to my old man one day,

'Dad, why can't we be Jews?' And he said,

'Because we're Roman Catholics,' and I said,

'Well we picked the wrong religion.' What could you expect? The old man was like that – a born loser – he always picked the wrong dogs, the wrong horses, the wrong side of town to live. He believed in God but I've a feeling that God didn't believe in him, that was the trouble.

Eric Sykes was my image of what a successful writer should look like. Expensive camel hair overcoat, a half-smoked cigar and an air of easy-come, easy-go. The same description would fit a bookmaker, but that's by the way.

Up until I met Eric I always thought that scriptwriters carried briefcases, but I realise now that they were only for insurance men and other dodgy characters. Eric always carried his scripts stuffed in the pocket of this camel hair overcoat. The real pro who knew that if he lost it there was more where that came from – out of his inventive mind. Even till this day, scriptwriters with briefcases I always view with suspicion and deep distrust, because either they have nicked the script or they have taken so long to write it or collect it that they need to keep it under lock and key because if they lose it – disaster – there ain't no more where that came from, because where that came from the fellow now locks up his filing cabinet.

The mark of a real pro is a contempt for the equipment he works with because he knows that the real equipment that makes him different from the rest is in his mind.

Sam Snead could beat the average golfer round any course he cared to name with one club whittled from the branch of a tree, and a driving range golf ball. He actually started playing golf with one club whittled from the branch of a tree and shot a round on a neighbouring course in the low seventies – barefoot. He may use Slazengers now but he knows he could do equally well with Dunlop, and plays with the product of whoever pays him most.

It's like the first great photographer I met. My wife had just bought a Pentax – her pride and joy – but he had *five* and treated them like a load of rubbish, throwing them with a clunk back into his bag when he had finished with them. He carried five of them to save him reloading or changing lenses. One day he *had* to change a lens and picking up one of the cameras said,

'Look at this – it's bloody bent.' I said,

'It's the way you throw them into the bag, I suppose.' He said,

'That's not the point – they shouldn't bend that easy.'

My first employment as a writer was for a show called *Mr Ros and Mr Ray*. Mr Ros and Mr Ray were Edmundo Ros and Ray Ellington, two bandleaders who not only couldn't act, they could hardly talk proper. So any big words would have been lost, not only on their audiences but on them as well. And as the BBC didn't pay you any more for big words it seemed best to stick with the little ones. It was more economical because they took up less room on the paper.

I never had a lot of time for big words. They're harder to spell for one thing and if you stutter like I do they're harder to speak as well. I always try to slip out little words before my stutter notices them.

Of course this was a handicap for a writer because only being able to use little words which everyone could understand, I had to be very careful what I said. I couldn't hide behind an indecipherable display of semantics. I was out in the open, and on my own, with no dictionary to protect me. Also I quickly began to realise that Edmundo Ros and Ray Ellington weren't extraordinary in their ignorance of big words. Then again perhaps they weren't all that ignorant but merely thought that you were – the audience, and the way some of those early audiences responded to my gags I'm not sure they weren't right.

Anyway, all that apart, I didn't know any big words, and so couldn't have used them if I'd wanted to. I was only just starting and I hadn't got around to a dictionary yet. I hadn't got round to a Smart & Weston suit yet either, and also I figured that most radio audiences were ordinary, simple people like my Mum and Dad, and that a simple lad like myself with a simple gift for simple words might have a warm-hearted appeal for them. I thought this could be my gimmick. Homespun philosophic humour written in simple four letter words. Of course some of the four-letter words couldn't be used in those days.

I did buy a dictionary in search of euphemism, the Concise Oxford Dictionary. It was a large book and I thought, 'I'll never get this home on the tube in the rush hour,' and said,

'Have you got a shorter one?'

He said, 'Yes, but it's bigger.'

So I said to him, 'If it's bigger why is it called the Shorter Oxford Dictionary?'

And he said, 'Well, I don't know, do I? I only sell it – I don't make it!'

I said, 'Have you got a smaller one?'

He said, 'Yes, but not in the Shorter edition. We've got a Pocket edition.'

I said, 'I'll have that one then.'

He said, 'Do you wear glasses?'

I said, 'No.'

He said, 'There's a bloke round the corner who makes good glasses – here's his card.'

I said, 'But I don't need glasses.'

He said, 'You will if you want to read that.'

So I kept my money and bought a tie in Smart & Westons. 'Well,' I thought, 'if they don't know the difference between shorter and bigger I'm not going to get value there.' So I stuck to my little words and shuffled them round a bit more. And when you think that ninety per cent of the people of the world are semi-illiterate and this was the BIG audience I wanted to attract, I couldn't see the sense in lugging big words about when all they wanted was the little ones.

I mean, God didn't use any big words when He wrote the Bible, did He? – and His book sold well. Even if He hadn't been God – with His royalties He could have lived like God anyway – and I didn't want to get bigger than Him. I mean that's the top – He's up there with Harold Robbins and Mickey Spillane. I bet He doesn't wear a Smart & Weston suit. I met Him in Harrods once, God. He was trying to cash a cheque. They wouldn't wear it. Well, would you cash a cheque for anyone who said he was God and was drawing on The Bank of Heaven? They had no doubt he was a nut even though he was wearing a Chester Barrie suit.

He said to me, 'The trouble with me – I haven't got a known face.'

I said, 'You ought to do more television,' and added, 'Is that Mick Jagger one of your lads? There's a resemblance.'

He said, 'No – none of my family'd come down here any more – not after that last business!'

So I said, 'Yeah – nasty that was – must have ruined your Easter!'

He was a good writer though. There was a man who knew the power of the written word. He must have shouted Himself hoarse telling Moses and the Israelites how to run the world. He probably went blue in the face. Well, some people you can talk to and it goes in one ear and out the other. The only way to make them take notice is to write it down in great big print.

So GOD took Moses up a mountain and wrote the ten commandments on ten big stones and made him carry them down to the waiting Israelites, and I suppose God thought to himself, 'If that doesn't sink in – nothing will.' God should have hit the Israelites over the head with those bloody stones – because what He wrote on them hasn't sunk in yet!

Anyway, with little words poking out of my new Smart & Weston suit I took myself off to the BBC to write the *Ros and Ray Show* which had been dreamed up by one of the BBC's bright boys to replace the *Billy Cotton Band Show* – and after a forgettable run of twelve weeks (I think the only three people who remember it are me, Edmundo Ros and Ray Ellington, and they'd probably prefer to forget it anyway, and won't take too kindly to my bringing it up now. But like the prisoner in the dock I think this might be a good time to get all my offences taken into consideration) – Billy Cotton came back and went on for ever. Which pleased my old man because he preferred the *Billy Cotton Band Show* anyway.

He said to me one day during the run of Ros and Ray,

'So you get paid for all that?'

I said, 'Yeah.'

He said, 'That BBC must have more money than sense.'

I took him up to the BBC Club one day at the TV Centre, Wood Lane, and he said to me:

'How much did this building cost?' and I said, 'Millions.'

And he looked round the crowded bar and said,

'Still, I suppose the bar pays for it don't it?'

He wasn't far wrong because when I stopped drinking they were forced to cancel two shows.

Shortly after Ros and Ray, I went on to write the Frankie Howerd Show, with Dick Barrie, Terry Nation and John Antrobus.

Frank is a great comedian, one of the best I've worked with and I've worked with most – he managed to make those little words sound like big ones. 'You don't have to write all those Ooooh-aaahs in,' he said, 'I'll put those in myself.'

I thought, 'Ah! this one can ad lib.'

I look at some of those scripts now and I must say, thanks to Frank we got away with murder. He's a marvellous avuncular character and was like a father to us.

The first show we wrote for him sounded dull, flat and completely unfunny during rehearsals. I was worried and remarked on how bad it sounded to Dick Barrie who took another bite at his apple, looked at Frank and said, 'He's probably saving a lot for tonight.' I said incredulously, 'What – gags?' He said, 'Well, he ain't put his own stuff in yet.' One of the others said, 'He's saving his performance for tonight.' It was my first lesson that some performers don't give their all at rehearsals. Somebody else said,

'He won't start being funny till the audience come in.' I looked at him in amazement and said,

'But that's our script he's reading.'

'Yeah, but he's not working it yet.'

They seemed to think he was going to produce some miraculous performance – I had never felt so depressed. I had friends coming to see the show and I wasn't looking forward to an embarrassing evening. I went across to the pub and began to get stoned.

I thought to myself, 'The insurance business isn't that bad, and they said I could always go back if I want to and anyway this wasn't the stuff I wanted to write. I was better at plays, and besides I should have stayed on my own. These three could hold me back.'

Then I thought, 'One of my lines got a laugh this afternoon.' I remembered now, it was the actor who spoke it – he'd laughed – he'd even asked Frank not to cut it. I remember him moaning he only had three lines and two of them had been cut already.

I got another large Scotch. A crowd of people came in to have a drink before going to the show. You could tell they were a BBC audience. I don't know where the BBC get their audiences from. They're not good audiences, they're rubbish most of them. Just like all their props, they don't work.

'Look at them over there,' I thought, 'all happy and smiling – they don't know what they're in for – serve them right.'

I thought, 'They won't be like that for long.' I started to hate them. I thought, 'It's people like that who'll get me the sack. If they don't laugh I could get the push – and it's back to the insurance. Just because a thick BBC audience don't think you're funny you could be out of work. I mean, how am I supposed to know what they think is funny? I'm not God. If I was I'd give them a rough time – BBC audiences – I'd give 'em comedy shows. I'd want to know why they weren't in church for a start – it was Sunday – Bloody Easter too! Good Friday hardly over and they're out looking for a laugh already.'

There was a vicar with them as well – what's he doing in a pub? He was a Roman Catholic priest too – I could tell that by his red face, his bloodshot eyes and the large Scotch in his hand. I bet he don't use wine for the Holy Communion – more like pink gins. I don't know why God puts up with 'em. If I was Him I'd sack the lot of 'em. A hard day's work would do him good – the fat slob – prying into other people's sins – sitting in the bloody confessional box.

'Did you indulge these bad thoughts my boy?'

'Soppy sod – course I did – wouldn't have them otherwise.'

'Did they involve men or women?'

What does he think I am, a bloody queer? I bet he is – he's not supposed to have women but they don't say nothing about choir boys.

'You must try not to have bad thoughts.'

'Why not, it's all I do get – I haven't had a bird for months.'

'Say four "Our Fathers" and three "Hail Marys".'

Christ, that's a lot for a few bad thoughts – I wonder what Bridget Murphy got when she told him she'd been poked? I bet she's still on her bloody knees.

The audience started to move away. I thought, 'Oh well, I'd better face it.' As I left the pub I saw my friends arriving.

'What's the show like?' one of them said.

'It's a good script,' I said defiantly, implying that any failure was down to Frank.

The show started with this prissy announcer in a tatty dress suit saying, 'It's the *Frankie Howerd Show!*' and then, to the music of his signature tune *You Can't Have Everything* (I thought – tonight he's not kidding) he started and it was a riot from beginning to end.

How he did it I don't know.

13 The longest play in the world

So we went on to write several series with Frankie Howerd, then the team split up and we all went our different ways. In the ensuing year I wrote for (apart from Frank) Peter Sellers, Morecambe & Wise, Arthur Askey, Cyril Fletcher, Vic Oliver, and others well known only to their families and immediate friends.

The first comic I met who allowed me to write in my own style was Arthur Haynes. I mean this in no derogatory way to other comedians but they were all already established personalities with a marked style that was individually them, whereas Arthur was completely unknown to the growing hordes of television viewers and I was able, to some extent, to create characters that he could portray, i.e. his tramp, or various know-all working-class types bucking against the rules created by authority, to keep you in the place where they preferred you to be, i.e. down a coalmine or at a work bench or in a dole queue, or if you were amoral enough, aping your betters and pursuing a life of crime, trailing light-years behind the big villains of industry, but nevertheless nicking a crust. Arthur Haynes was one of the first truly great television comedians. With Arthur there was no over-emphasis in performance – he seemed to do it all with his eyes, and when he played a character, he gave the impression that he had just walked in off the street. His art really concealed his art.

It was a great relationship – he knew the characters as I knew them. The only limitations I had as a writer were engendered by a silly convention that because he was Arthur Haynes, and it was the Arthur Haynes Show, there was a danger that anything he said in character would be taken out of character and attributed to Arthur Haynes the TV personality, i.e. if Arthur, portraying a typical working-class character, had referred to coloured people as 'them coons' and 'nignogs' in the way that say Alf Garnett does, he could have had the stigma of racial prejudice attached to his own name. Whereas when Alf Garnett says it, no blame can be attached to Warren Mitchell, the actor who portrays him. In the mind of the public Warren Mitchell and Alf Garnett lead completely separate lives, whereas the public could have quite often, stupidly I concede, not been able to differentiate between Arthur and the character he was portraying.

As a writer I found this becoming more and more irritating and wanted more and more to delineate characters who would take the blame for their own abysmal ignorance and bigoted prejudice, i.e. the man in the street or in the Big House or the pretentious middle-class box who are responsible for some of the most stupid utterances of our time on race, religion, philosophy and politics.

More and more I wanted to write plays, and one evening I came home seething with frustration, despising my own inability to write, hating myself for not being able to fulfil the functions that I knew a writer must fulfil – chronicling all around him including self.

I said to my wife who was happily ironing at the time, 'I think I'm just a Chekhov character – one of those people who's always going on about what he can do and can't do, and then does nothing.'

She said, 'Your dinner's in the oven.'

I said, 'I want to write a play.'

And she said, 'Well no one's stopping you.'

I said, 'Oh, you don't understand – and before you put those shirts in the airing cupboard make sure there's buttons on them. There was no button on this shirt this morning.'

I said, 'You're daft you are – you wash shirts and iron them and then put them in the airing cupboard with no buttons on them.'

I said, 'There's no point is there? You can't wear shirts when there's no buttons on them.'

She said, 'Sew your own buttons on.'

I said, 'You're a big help you are – I want to write a play.'

And she said, 'I want to finish this ironing without a lot of aggro.'

I said, 'I'm a Chekhov character that's what I am – right out of the *Cherry Orchard*.'

I said, 'That play's not a comedy – it's a bloody tragedy! It's not a Russian play – it's about us! Chekhov wasn't writing about a bloody Cherry Orchard – it was England, the world – and he's got us all in it – bloody hell!'

I'd had some ideas about a play idling about in my mind and so I got out my typewriter, put some paper in it and started to write. My wife went to bed and the fire went out, but I was so engrossed I didn't notice. And a bottle of Remy Martin that was on a side table got empty. It was suddenly dawn and I realised I was cold; I had twenty-eight sheets of closely typed paper, an empty Remy Martin bottle – I was cold sober and exhausted. I thought, 'It's probably a load of old crap,' and went to bed. I must say I really felt better but wasn't daring to hope.

In the morning my wife Connie read what I had written and thought it was marvellous so I took it into the office and showed it to John Antrobus who went wild about it. This was the play that became *The Compartment*.

Excited and in a state of near delirium by Antrobus raving about the play and wanting to hear more of this heady and enthusiastic praise of it I took him to lunch in the very expensive Chinese restaurant, Fu Tong in the High Street, Kensington, and ordered the lot. Cold wine, hot saki ... During this meal Peter Sellers and his wife came and sat at the next table and Peter remarked on a revue *The Art of Living* that I had contributed to, and said he thought that my sketches were the best stuff in it.

What with that and John still babbling about *The Compartment* and the hot saki . . . I was well up on Cloud Nine. Peter asked me what I was doing at the moment and I said, with an attempt at studied casualness, that I'd just written a play, and paused for John to say 'A great play', which he didn't. Anyway Peter asked to see the play. He said he was thinking of doing something on television in America – and the way it sounded it might suit his needs. Well, plus that and the cold wine and the hot saki and the brandies that Antrobus was now demanding, I was too excited to eat. There was all that marvellous expensive food – those marvellous prawns, the succulent spare ribs, the sweet and sour, the special fried rice, the chunks of lobster and I was too overcome to eat any of it.

When I got back to the office I sent the play to Peter and he 'phoned the next morning to say it was wonderful and one of the funniest things he'd ever read which started me off again and led to me not being able to eat a meat pudding, my favourite dish that my wife Connie had prepared specially for me – I was losing pounds and I thought, 'Too much success like this and I will end up like something out of Belsen.'

Peter wanted to buy the play and do it in America but I wanted it done in England by the BBC, who we now knew also wanted to do it. I suppose I thought with some strange idiotic reasoning that if Peter bought it and did it in America I'd never see it performed, whereas if I could persuade him to do it for the BBC I could sit at home and watch it. Peter agreed to do it for the BBC but there was always another film, and finally Elwyn Jones, who was then acting Head of Drama, 'phoned me and asked if they could do it with someone else as they really wanted to get it on the air, and they had an actor in mind who they thought would be ideal in the part and would I come and hear him read. Well – he only read a couple of pages and I said, 'That's it – he's marvellous.' And that was Michael Caine, who also did my next play *The Playmates*.

I had now got the bug for playwriting and wrote my first three-act play *The Knacker's Yard*, which was staged at the Arts Theatre (where although it was a Club theatre we were censored) with Dermot Kelly, Maxwell Shaw and Marjorie Laurence, and directed by that well-known Irish rebel of the theatre, Alan Simpson. This is where I met Dermot who later became the other tramp with Arthur Haynes.

The notices for the play were mixed. Those who liked it – and there were many – loved it, and those who hated it – and there were equally many – loathed it. I don't mind a critic pointing out that my work is of feeble construction and that it lacks concept and style and that other word so loved these days – structure, or that it's poorly written and without any real grasp of language, as long as he's not using these defects as a stick just to beat the ideas with. And also as long as he knows what he's talking about. Leave out all the nit-picking brouhaha and stick to the questions: is it good theatre, does it work, is it exciting, and if it's a comedy, is it funny? The audience may not be intellectuals but they know funny when they see it. We have a phrase peculiar to this country: 'gentle comedy,' which I've always found to mean not very funny, but almost always very boring. Comforting comedy is what they mean, I suppose, by gentle comedy. Caring comedy. The New Wave, Alternative comedy, which as far as I can see, sets out, not only not to attack our appalling prejudices and awful bigotry, but to assuage our prim National propriety by declining to notice them. I don't even really mind being called an illiterate guttersnipe, as an irate critic once labelled me. It doesn't cause me any loss of sleep. Snipe I do, I suppose, and dragged up out of the gutter I was. I'm one of those Englishmen who, as Shaw says, has only to open his mouth to be despised by other Englishmen.

I remember arriving at the Imperial Hotel, Torquay, driving my Rolls. Connie, my wife, was sitting in the back with the kids. As the car drew to a stop, the doorman rushed up saluting and opened the door for them. Ah, people of substance, the quality, you could see what he was thinking as he helped them out of the car. It was like a dog wagging its tail at the master's return. An icon of subservient gratitude.

As I went to follow them, carrying our bags, he grabbed them from me.

'I'll take these,' he said brusquely. He'd heard me speak and thought I was the chauffeur and didn't want me walking into the hotel, at least, not through the front door.

'I'm staying here, I gotta sign in,' I said. He looked at the Rolls, and then back at me. He couldn't link the two, and was very confused. He was embarrassing me a bit too, and making me feel a bit flash. So I gave him ten quid, pointed to the luggage still in the boot and said,

'If you can get this up to the room, eh?' He took the money but with a gesture that made me feel even more flash. Ten pounds was a lot of money in those days; it's a lot of money today, but it was even more then, and this was an act of gross over-tipping, something only a person as badly brought up as I was would be guilty of. And he knew that. He also knew that, Rolls-Royce or no Rolls-Royce, ten pounds or no ten pounds, I was a guttersnipe. Dogs and children and hotel door keepers can sniff out a bum, so the saying goes. My own dogs and children have adjusted to me, it seems, but they still show more respect to my wife.

These days, hotel door keepers have got more used to guttersnipes driving around in Rolls-Royces, most of our pop stars for a start, and nearly all of our modern millionaires are ex-guttersnipes who most likely grossly over-tip. I've got a sneaking suspicion that most hotel door keepers are not too keen on this change in things and would much rather still be serving the more genteel who speak and behave like ladies and gentlemen even if they're not. The gross over-tipping I'm sure they've managed to adjust to more easily.

I had an adventure in my Rolls with a tramp, who provided me with a wonderful character for Arthur Haynes. I was stopped at traffic lights one day when the door of the car was opened and this tramp climbed in.

Before I could do or say anything the lights changed and I had to move on.

'This a Rolls?' the tramp said, adjusting the sun visor. 'Prefer 'em,' he said, 'you meet a better class of people in 'em. I've been waiting there awhile, I've let a lot of the rubbish go by.' He fiddled under the dash and then said, 'Cocktail cabinet?'

'I haven't got one,' I said.

'Should have a cocktail cabinet in a car like this,' he said.

'I don't drink when I'm driving,' I said.

'Shouldn't have to drive a Rolls if you own it,' he said. 'These cars are made for a servant to drive. All the comforts in the back. Yer cocktail cabinet, yer telephone, yer fax, all that,' he said, 'all that's in the back for yer gentleman to use. I mean,' he went on, 'people who buy these cars don't have all that expensive education at Eton an' Harrow just to end up driving a car, I mean, that's not a gentleman's job, driving a car, specially a posh car like this. I mean, that's an underling's job. You'll never see the Queen drive herself, or any of yer nobs.'

'Well, I'm not one of yer nobs,' I said.

'Oh, I know that,' he said, 'I can tell that ... no offence.' Someone else who knew a guttersnipe when he heard one.

'You must have a few bob though, eh?' he said. 'I mean, running one of these must cost a few bob, eh?' I nodded. I was beginning to realise my good fortune in meeting this character. He was a gift. He was going to cost me a few bob I suspected, but I didn't mind.

'Yer, must cost a bit to run, one of these,' he nodded sagely, 'a good few bob I reckon.' A pause and then, 'I'm trying get down to Southend,' he said. 'Not going that way, are yer?'

As we were at that moment proceeding along the A40 in the direction of White City, I don't think he was expecting a yes from me. And even if I had been going anywhere near Southend I don't think he imagined I would volunteer the information and invite him to stay with me. He wasn't daft. He knew he wasn't anyone's idea of a travelling companion. Especially someone driving a Rolls, even if he was an ex-guttersnipe. In fact, it might sound awful, but I was beginning to worry more about his unsavoury arse on the seat of my smart Rolls than I was about his welfare or how he would get to Southend or anywhere else for that matter. The smell he was giving off was also conjuring up thoughts of how to get rid of him. I'd got enough out of him. He'd sparked off in me the idea of a great character for Arthur to play. After all I was a comedy writer, and the job of a comedy writer is to transpose the misfortunes of others into cathartic, hilarious merriment for the rest of us, while making a few bob for himself. And, because of this not altogether altruistic motive, but I had a family to keep, *Till Death Us Do Part* carried on.

The way Alf started was like this: round about the time I was beginning to write plays, Dennis Main-Wilson, a unique kind of madman that the BBC seemed to specialise in (and without whom they would not be able to properly function – they're its life blood in many ways) asked me to write a half-hour Comedy Playhouse which became *Till Death Us Do Part*. It was amazingly successful and since then fifteen other series have been produced, altogether running for twenty-five years (making it Britain's longest running comedy show).

Two films about the Garnetts were made that broke box office records and were successful in American art houses, but were never put out there on general release. It was the language difficulty they claimed. Americans apparently can't understand English when it's spoken by English actors.

An American changed-format production based on *Till Death Us Do Part*, called *All In The Family*, was unleashed on the American public, starring Carol O'Connor, Jean Stapleton, Bob Reiner, and Sally Struthers. O'Connor played Archie Bunker, the Alf equivalent. It became an instant success, won innumerable awards, was voted the best comedy show in thirty years and led Frank Sinatra – his show was knocked out of the ratings by it – to say, 'So, it's bigots they want now!'

Back on this side of the Atlantic, Warren and I did a one-man show – or rather Warren did the show, I wrote it – called *The Thoughts Of Chairman Alf* for which I picked up the *Evening Standard* Drama Award for best comedy.

And then, at the instigation of Dandy Nichols, we did a changed format with just Warren and Dandy, called *In Sickness and in Health*. No family any more, just these two old people, Alf and his long suffering Silly Old Moo, with the Silly Old Moo really suffering now, confined to a wheelchair, but Alf, I suspect, suffering more from having to push it. It was another instant success, praised by the critics, loved by the public, and with Alf becoming something of a folk hero as he battled with the bureaucrats of the DSS, and tried to keep body and soul together on the miserly State pension.

But still I had my critics, some of them still quite venomous, although not the fascists of the earlier days who spelled out their vile abuse of me and Warren with capital letters cut from newspapers, and referred to me as 'You Jewboy' obviously a term intended to be derogatory, although I am unable to accept 'Jew' as an insult, and 'boy' at my age is a forgotten memory. But to these sick minds it was foul abuse. As far as I know, I am of Irish descent, but as I was born in England, I call myself English. That's what it says on my passport, although in some parts of the world, it might be more convenient if it said something else.

Most of these liberal zealots, who attack me and my writing with such fundamentalist fervour, appear to lack any kind of subtlety of mind. They miss the satire entirely, and blame me, as if I had endowed Alf Garnett, and other characters I may write, with all the unpleasantness they reveal. It seems they would prefer me not to draw attention to the nastier, more disagreeable side of people. They would prefer, if I must draw my characters from life, not to draw them with warts and all. How they expect me, or any other writer, to record truthfully all those bigoted, illiberal chauvinists and other xenophobic half-wits that plague us, without showing them in full cry, is beyond me. Never mind, eh? You can't please 'em all.

The idea is to try and write good, believable characters. To try and lift them right off the street with all their silly prejudices and other more major blemishes, and present them in a theatrical frame . . . here you are, this is what we're like . . . or some of us at least. What helps the playwright to put his ideas across is the casting of good actors, and the best way to get good actors, is to offer them very good parts – or very good money. What keeps Shakespeare alive, I would venture at the risk of abuse, is not the poetry but the great acting parts. Great actors through the ages want to play them. If he had written novels instead of plays, no matter how good the poetry, he wouldn't be so vivid and part of our age as he still is. If he was alive though I bet he'd be getting threatening letters.

The Queen Mum was threatened not to attend the Royal Command Performance at which Alf Garnett was to appear. She told me so herself in the line-up. She had heard that I'd been threatened for writing it.

'Don't worry,' she said, 'they're only cranks.'

'It's only cranks I worry about, ma'am,' I said. 'It's only cranks who do those kind of things.' The ordinary, normal people are no problem. Some of them make lousy audiences – they don't laugh loud and long enough at some of my shows, but that's my only objection.

While I'm dropping Royal names I might as well mention meeting Prince Philip. This was at the last of the Goon Shows, a right Royal bash I must say, with most of them there in attendance, and those that weren't sending goony telegrams to Spike and Peter. I was about to be introduced to Prince Philip by Con Mahoney, one of sound radio's bigwigs, when Peter Sellers pulled me away. Mahoney had just said, 'And this is Johnny Speight, sir, the creator of . . . ' when Peter grabbed me by the arm and yanked me away.

What do you do in situations like that? I froze. And then Peter released me, and Con Mahoney, with amazing BBC aplomb and composure, carried on with the introduction as though nothing untoward had happened.

'This is Johnny Speight, sir, the creator of *Till Death Us Do Part.*' I was gone, confused, and thrown out of my stride completely. I bowed low, and subservient as any peasant has ever been in the presence of Royalty, scraping the floor with my outstretched hand almost, said,

'Pleased to meet you your Majesty.' All wrong. And Philip replied,

'I'm not a dwarf.' I straightened myself up, abashed hardly describes my feelings, and Prince Philip introduced me to

Princess Anne as, 'This is the gentleman who writes your mother's favourite show.' Well, that made up for a bit. Lord Mountbatten liked Alf too, and as Prince Charles told Una Stubbs, Lord Louis never went out while the show was on. *Till Death* was always popular with the Royals. Well, as Frank Muir said once, we were doing a very good PR job on them with Alf advocating that the Queen should sack Parliament and run the country herself.

14 On to meeting two of America's showbusiness royalty

After meeting blue-blooded royalty I was now, without knowing it, headed towards meeting what is called showbusiness royalty. Two great, then living, legends. They say any fool can become a king and many do, but to become a king of showbusiness requires a fair amount of extra special, really outstanding, talent and both of these had much more than the minimum needed to impress their peers.

I was staying in Scotland on one occasion at the Gleneagles Hotel, playing golf, and my son Francis, who was very young at the time, and already a better golfer than I would ever be, came into our room and said,

'Dad, there's a famous American golfer here ... he's called Boing Krisby ... d'you know him? His bag's downstairs,' said Francis, 'it's got his name on it.' Of course, it was the hall porter's broad Scottish accent that produced Boing Krisby. The golf bag standing in the hotel foyer belonged to Bing Crosby, his name written on it in large white letters.

During that week at Gleneagles, every time I saw him, he had a gaping crowd in tow, a good many of them walking backwards in front of him taking his picture from all sorts of angles with all sorts of holiday cameras, some of the bolder, or more insensitive ones, cheekily posing him, 'One with Mum and Aunt Maud ... one with Pa ... one with the kids ... ' And he took all this with the most amazing charm and fortitude, joking with them, and acting up to their suggestions without the slightest show of impatience. Lesser stars I know would have run for cover plaintively whining, 'No, no, not now, I'm busy!' They say the bigger they are the nicer and more courteously they behave. One of the girls at BBC Reception told me,

'The big stars are no problem. It's the jumped-up little sodding nothings that give you a pain!' I was with Richard Burton in the Savoy one day and the manager came up and said,

'It's pissing down outside and there's two thousand of 'em out there waiting, d'you want me to smuggle you out to your car?' And Burton said,

'No, they buy the tickets, it's their bums on seats that bought the car, I'll go out that way,' and he pointed to where the fans were waiting. I watched him stand in the rain signing autographs, the rain dripping down his face. They don't come much bigger than he was either.

Anyway, Boing Krisby was in the hotel, and Francis must have been one of the few people in the world who didn't know who he was. They say it doesn't matter how big you are, there's always someone, somewhere in the world, who doesn't know who you are, and what's more, they don't give a shit! Francis began to lose interest in Bing once he learned he wasn't a famous American golfer. But I was ... agog is the word! He was the first singer I'd heard who sang my kind of music with a jazzy beat, him and Louis Armstrong; then came Billie Holliday, Ella Fitzgerald, Sinatra, the great big band singers; this was my culture, the only culture I knew in those days. It was jazz! And here he was in the Gleneagles Hotel and I wanted to meet him. But how?

I'd argued with my father over Bing Crosby. He was contemptuous of him. Like Alf was contemptuous of Van Gogh and Mozart.

'He can't sing,' my father used to say. 'You can't call that singing, all that boopy doopy doop! He has to have a microphone, you wouldn't hear him if it wasn't for that!' My father liked his singers loud, and a drunken uncle singing *Danny Boy* or *The Mountains Of Mourne* could bring a tear to his eyes, but Bing

Crosby, Frank Sinatra, or Ella left him unmoved. Good phrasing and tone had no appeal to him. But there you go, all art is a matter of taste, and they weren't to his taste. He didn't have a lot of time for Shakespeare either, and didn't feel in the least deprived because he hadn't read Shelley or Keats. Even Sir Thomas Beecham with all his putative appeal to the masses didn't reach my father. The only Beechams he knew were the ones who made the powders.

Eric Sykes phoned me the day after Bing arrived in the hotel; I told him all about it and how I'd like to meet him, and he said,

'Well go and say hello to him.'

'You can't do that,' I said, 'not to a big star like that.'

'He's a nice guy,' Eric said, 'he won't mind.' I knew he was a nice guy. I'd seen him with all those crowds, something I wouldn't have fancied to be honest, and how forbearing he was with them.

'All right,' I said, 'if I say a mutual friend of ours told me to . . .'

'No!' said Eric, and put the phone down. I rang him back.

'Why don't you come up here to Scotland, Eric,' I said, 'you could do with some fresh air, and you could introduce me.'

'Piss off!' Eric said, before he put the phone down again.

And then Bing came into the cocktail bar. Connie and the kids had gone into lunch, and I was having a livener, well, you know, an aperitif. All right, having a few before lunch. It was in the days when I drank, and I drank quite a bit. Francis was standing in the doorway waiting for me, like he always did. As I did when I was a kid, standing outside the pub, looking in, hoping my father would fetch an arrowroot biscuit out for me, or shouting in for a lemonade, or, 'You gonna be long, Dad?' He was a forbearing man too.

Bing walked into the bar and came straight over to me, his hand outstretched, and said,

'Johnny Speight? Bing Crosby. Can I call you Johnny?'

I said, 'Yeah,' or something of that sort, 'can I call you Bing?'

'You got a great show in our backyard,' he said. He meant *All In The Family*. Frannie went rushing into the dining room shouting,

'Mummy! Mummy! Daddy's drinking with Boing Krisby!'

Later during the week, Connie woke me one morning, all excited, saying,

'Listen, it's Bing, he's singing.' He was in the next room to us, so I said,

'Well, bang on the wall!' He was one of the first really great stars I had met. And he was exactly as I imagined him. I've heard several tales about him since, things in various books and news-papers, but all I have to say is, when I met him he struck me, as Eric Sykes said, as a really nice guy.

Now I'd met Bing, I got to meet the friend who was travelling with him, a guy they called Mr Pineapple. I never found out his real name but apparently he grew most of the world's pineapples. Little did I know when I lived in Canning Town that one day I'd be sitting drinking with the guy who grew all those pineapples we ate at teatime on Sunday nights. Winkles and pineapple with custard. (A posh tea in those far-off days. Bob Monkhouse's family were responsible for the custard I believe.) This Mr Pine-apple came from Hawaii and was the wealthiest man I'd ever met until then, he probably still is. He had two luxurious stretch limos he'd brought across with him, and they stood parked outside the hotel all week, complete with smartly uniformed chauffeurs, wait-ing his command, and they never moved, not once, not all week. Those two chauffeurs stood by those cars from nine in the morn-ing till seven at night just on the off chance he might need them. He never did. But, there you are, that's what serious money is all about, I suppose, being able to keep hordes of people standing around trying to anticipate every whim, and minister to every small need you may have. I heard that his entourage occupied two floors of the hotel and half the village down the road. I don't know if he wiped his own arse, and screwed his own wife, but if he did, they were the only things he did for himself. He lived on a much more lavish scale than Bing, and Bing couldn't have been short of a few bob.

I walked into the cocktail bar one evening and he was sitting at a table by himself.

'Hey,' he called, 'Johnny, sit down.' I sat down and he said,

'Whadaya wanna drink?' They sold champagne by the glass at Gleneagles, so I said,

'I'll have a glass of champagne if you don't mind.' He turned to call a waiter but the waiter was a couple of beats in front of him.

'Yes, sir,' he said, 'a glass of champagne for Mr Speight.'

A glass of champagne in those days, in that best of all the five-star hotels in Europe (Prime Ministers stayed there, at least Tory Prime Ministers stayed there), was one pound twenty a glass. (Inflation will never get to be that low again, no matter who runs the country.) The waiter brought the champagne, and Mr Pineapple stuck a fiver in the top pocket of his serving coat.

'Keep the change,' he said. A few minutes later and Connie, my wife, arrived in the bar and sat down with us.

'Whadaya wanna drink, Connie?' asked Mr Pineapple. Connie saw I was drinking champagne so she said,

'Oh, er ... champagne please.'

'Yes, Mrs Speight,' said our friendly and attentive waiter. When he returned with the champagne, Mr Pineapple stuffed another fiver into the pocket of his coat. And this is how it went on. Bing, joined us, another fiver in the waiter's pocket. Some other people, more fivers ... then Mrs Pineapple came into the bar and when our getting-richer-by-the-minute waiter saw her, he threw his arms out in an histrionic, welcoming gesture, rather like a caricature of an old-time thespian.

'Ah!' he exclaimed melodramatically, really over the top he was, 'and what vision of loveliness have we here?' (He could probably see fivers sticking out all over her.) All delivered in a broad Gorbals accent. More champagne, another fiver. He was making more than the hotel was making. Out of their one pound twenty, they had to buy the champagne. I'd like to know what Karl Marx would have made of that. I wondered if Securicor took him home at night. I found myself avoiding Mr Pineapple after that. Well, he wouldn't let anyone else buy a drink. He made me feel uncomfortable, and very poor.

The other great showbusiness legend, Sammy Davis jnr, didn't have anything like the kind of serious money Mr Pineapple had, but his extravagance with what he did have, was, although on a par with Mr Pineapple, a more easy come, easy go, attitude. It was a more colourful, celebratory stance. I mean, let's face it, Sammy didn't have to impress anybody with his money, and everyone in his presence knew it. His talent was enough.

I first met Sammy Davis some years back when he was appearing nightly at the Grosvenor Hotel in London. We met for lunch the week before he opened. Sammy was one of the world's great entertainers, a Mr Show Business, if ever there was one. He was an elegant, classy act, a vibrant personality, jazzy, witty, and rhythmic beyond belief – his dancing could make me laugh at its wit and beat and at the same time, put me into a state of pure elation at the cheeky impossibility of what he was doing with such consummate ease. He could seize and hold the rapt attention of an audience with everything he did, if it was only fooling around with a couple of six-guns, doing tricks with them, fast draw, spinning them, that John Wayne would have envied. And then of course there was his singing, and his voice stacked up well against the best.

It was an arranged lunch – he'd seen a play I'd written for TV, *The Compartment*, starring Michael Caine and Frank Finlay, and thought it was one of the best things he'd seen on TV – and wanted to talk about the possibility of me doing some TV with him. Yeah, well, why not . . . but I was just happy to meet him. He was the snappiest dresser I've ever met. His clothes reflected his jazzy persona, and were made of the finest materials, and cut with such style and flair – they were designer glitz before the term was coined. Well, I've always been a bit of a flash dresser myself (whenever I could afford the clothes and had the nerve to wear them), a result of the jazz days when I was struggling to be a musician, and Sammy was Mr Jazz, an icon of that exciting era I had so much wanted to be a part of, and the colourful clothes he wore with such casual unconcern were all part of his mythic charisma. He was the embodiment of the music I'd grown up with. Although I soon discovered the casual unconcern concealed a fastidious, very finicky trait in him of obsessive cleanliness and tidiness. Or perhaps it was to do with a show business fetish for

perfection, that state of feeling you look right, and ready to go on.
I heard that Frank Sinatra showers and changes five or six times a
day. Or maybe it's boredom when they're not on, like . . . what
shall I do now? I'll shower and change. Be ready. Anyway, on the
day I met him, the waiter knocked a glass of wine over him. And
lunch was halted while he went back to the hotel to change into a
another suit. Everything he changed, even the jewellery. I had to
sit there for over half an hour – he probably took a shower as well –
with people coming up saying

'Where's Sammy?'

'Oh, he's gone back to the hotel to change.'

I had another experience like that with the great Max Wall. In
Hanley, when I was just starting in the business, I had to meet
him to discuss a show, and he took me out to lunch. The waiter
brought the wine to the table, and in the time-honoured manner,
poured some into a glass and proffered it to Max to taste. Max
rolled the wine around his tongue, made a face, and spat it into
the waiter's face. As the red wine trickled down the waiter's face
and onto his white shirt-front, Max said with wonderful disdain,

'You should be locked up trying to sell filth like that.' And then
he rose from the table and did that funny walk of his out of the
restaurant, leaving me sitting there, terrified. I thought they'd
throw me out into the street. After a few moments he returned, sat
down, and said,

'Surely you must have something better?'

But to return to Sammy, the first words he said to me on that
day were,

'Hey, I just walked from the hotel, on my own, without a
bodyguard. What about that?' Well, I wasn't too impressed. I've
walked about London for years without a bodyguard. Most
Londoners walk about London without a bodyguard. I once saw
Paul Getty standing outside the Ritz Hotel without a bodyguard,
and he was a lot richer than Sammy. When you're born poor, you
go one or two ways, so they say. You either become very stingy, or
very extravagant. Sammy was very extravagant. He must have
been wearing more than a few thousand dollars worth of jewellery
about his person the day I met him. It chinked and rattled as he

moved. Moss Hart, the American playwright, used to be always buying apartments he didn't need, on the assumption that anyone who could spend that much money on real estate couldn't be poor. And Groucho Marx, at the other extreme, checked every shopping bill that came into the house, and would quite often do the shopping himself because he imagined he could strike harder bargains on the week's groceries than his wife could.

Sammy didn't bother to strike bargains. He seemed to spend his money as fast as he earned it, and worked very hard at earning more to stay in front. He had a whole floor for himself and his entourage at the Grosvenor, and threw champagne parties every night to large gatherings of celebrities. They weren't freeloaders, they were all big names, and with big thirsts some of them. Those parties every night must have set him back quite a bit. I don't know what he was earning at the Grosvenor, but I bet he didn't take much home with him.

After the first party – I was going to say first night party because it was the night the show opened, but every night of the run was like a first night – he invited me up to his suite. He came over to me and said, 'When you're through here, don't rush home, come up to the suite.' His show didn't start until about eleven, and it was now nearer two in the morning . . . so I don't know what he meant by don't rush home. I was tremendously flattered by how friendly he was to me. And very nervous. Let's face it, he was a big star, one of the world's great entertainers, and here he was acting buddies, treating me like an intimate, and I was scared of freezing, drying, and becoming tongue-tied. After all, here was another Mr Show Business, and me an illiterate guttersnipe. Although he wasn't out of the top drawer himself his start in life had been better than mine. His working life had started in vaudeville, mine had started in a spring-clip factory. He had been born into show business – there's a clip of film showing him hoofing it like a real pro at the age of three. Anyway, nervous or not, I was fascinated by him, by his superb talent, and was determined to visit his suite.

I went round to the front of the hotel and asked the hall porter where Sammy's suite was situated. Fortunately the hall porter recognised me and pointed to a lift.

'That one,' he said. 'That's Sammy's, it's private ... and guarded.'

'I've been invited up,' I said.

'You'll be all right then,' said the hall porter. 'So long as you've been invited. I wouldn't try it otherwise.'

I walked over to the lift, with a bit of trepidation I must say. I knew he had a bodyguard. I hadn't met them and I wasn't too keen to tangle with them at this time in the morning. But, nothing ventured ... so I pressed the lift button. The doors opened and standing in the lift were the two biggest black guys I'd ever seen. Either one of them could have given Mike Tyson a hard time.

One of them looked down at me and said,

'Yeah?' And my stutter started.

'Sssssss, sssss, sssss,' I started. He cut me short.

'What dya want?' he asked.

'Sssssssss ... Sa sa sa sa sa ... Oh, forget,' I said, and started to walk away.

'Hey, what's ya name?' he asked. I managed it, and he spoke into a phone.

'Tell Sammy there's a guy here ... Johnny Speight ... Yeah ...' He turned to me, 'Get in,' he said. I got in the lift. When we got to Sammy's floor there were more of them. Big muscular guys. Terrifying. Over the weeks I got to know them. They were great. Very friendly – if you were a friend of Sammy's.

Sammy didn't start till late as I say and went on till past two in the morning. One night I was in the cloakroom while he was on and the cloakroom attendant was furious.

'It's all right for him,' he said, meaning Sammy. 'He lives here. I gotta get home. It's all right for them,' meaning the audience, 'they've all got cars! I live at bloody Kilburn,' he went on, 'I gotta walk home!'

'Get a taxi,' I said.

'I can't afford no bloody taxis on what they pay me here,' he said. 'Most do's,' he said, 'they're out of here by half eleven, twelve the latest ... I can get a bus. But he don't come on till twelve an' no one knows what time he's gonna finish.'

'Well, he's popular,' I said.

'Not with me he ain't!' said the attendant with feeling. 'I tell you what,' he said, 'I'm gonna sod off here one night an' let 'em all sort their own coats out.' I told Sammy about this and he included it in the act. The audience loved it. So did the cloakroom attendant, especially when Sammy told the audience not to be cheapskates, and tip the man enough to get a taxi home.

15 Across the Atlantic to Hollywood

Going to America was quite an experience. There they really do take their show business seriously. It's big bucks as they say.

Whenever I've visited Hollywood it's always been at someone else's expense, which is really the best way to travel if you can work it. I've always been invited there because they think I may have something they can make some money out of. I'm always keen to accept their invites, because I know that if I've got something they can make some money out of, it will be big money, and I will make some big money too. So, as you can see, it's a mutually advantageous arrangement, plus the fact that they pay all my expenses. They fly me out first class, I'm met by a limo, and installed in one of their first class hotels. It's one of the things about American companies I admire most, if they want you, they don't penny pinch, they're not cheapskates.

And it's not just expenses they're willing to pay. If I have an idea that sounds like it might be a goer, they'll pay out all the seed money necessary to develop the idea, which means, in purely fiscal terms, they'll pay me a lot of money to write a pilot show. I can earn more in Hollywood writing a pilot than I would earn in England writing a series of seven shows.

Put another way this means I could live in a luxurious hotel suite in the Hollywood sunshine for a month or so, writing a pilot, for near enough the same as I would get to spend the winter in freezing London, working all hours to write a series. Why don't I do it? You may well ask. Especially as it's also a lot cheaper to live in America than it is to live in England. A good cigar will cost you two dollars there as against seven quid here, hotel rooms are cheaper, food and drink is cheaper and once you've bought the set, television is free. It's a highly competitive market and it appears to work to the benefit of the consumer at least.

Take computerware for example, I'm interested in that, and know a bit about it, the cost of it anyway. The American equivalent of a computer you could buy here would be half the cost and better, and the software to drive it the same. Which puts high technology comfortably within reach of the average American's pocket, so he uses it, and helps advance his society further in the technological race, whereas, here in England, because it's so expensive, we can't afford to use it, and so fall further behind. And where will it all end? In the poor house for most of us I think. We English are in danger of becoming the only people who can't afford to live in England. Very soon, I'm beginning to think, I may have to live in America, if only to earn enough money to carry on living in England.

Another reason I choose to live in England is that I like it here, and I like the people. It's home, and when I'm abroad, I can't wait to get back to it. But like all homes, it could be better run. Perhaps, we should get a Japanese government to run it for a while, you know, just till we get back in profit. It's amazing, Japan and Germany were both losers in World War Two ... but to look at them now you would think they won it. Perhaps that's what we should do, have another war with them, but this time make sure we lose. It's like someone in the Israeli Cabinet once said,

'If we wanna get rich, we should fight a war with a rich nation like America and lose it.' And someone else said,

'Yeah, but say we win?'

One other reason for not rushing off permanently to America, equally important as the others, is the need to have an idea they're willing to spend their kind of big money on. And, then of course, being able to pitch the idea to them successfully.

For those aspiring to make it in Hollywood as a writer, let me give you an idea of the kind of irritations you will come across on your way to making a fortune. First comes the pitch. Well, the idea comes first, but the pitch is the all-important bit. This is where you win or lose. And it's not easy. Because it seems to me, that only in the television industry (it may be the same in the film world – I don't know) is so much power given to those the least capable of handling it – people in fear of their jobs. And this is very much so in the American television industry. The people you pitch your script or idea to, have the power to say No, but not the power to say Yes. Well, they have the power to say Yes, but a No carries no commitment for them, whereas a Yes, unfortunately, triggers action and can put their job on the line. Scripts that are rejected are rejected in committee and never get past them to the next tier of authority. Scripts that are accepted are also accepted in committee, but if there's been a Yes, by the end of the meeting, as the result of some very clever manoeuvring, somebody will discover that he or she has been skilfully nominated and given all credit for the Yes, and is now solely responsible for its probable failure, thus absolving the rest of the committee from any possibility of blame.

Because many more shows fail than succeed, the vast majority in fact, this is not an enviable position to be in, and is very worrying for the committee man it happens to. He has been outwitted, singled from the pack, and is now on his own, with his young corporate head resting on the chopping block. Of course, he could get lucky. It could be a good idea, perhaps a great idea, with good writers behind it, good actors and a good director. The show could become a blockbusting success, and the victim could find himself the toast of the industry, the flavour of the month, sitting in a big house with a swimming pool, completely confused, and not knowing what the fuck happened. It is a bit like Vegas, it's the lucky who are the really big winners, not the clever professionals. This kind of power leads to the submission process nearly always favouring the acceptance of simple, recognizable

plots and characters and encourages the rejection of scripts dealing with complex ideas in an original way. And why not? It's an
insurance protection for the committee.

You may wonder how *All In The Family* with that arch-bigot
Archie Bunker ever got on the network? Well, some do get
through. But I bet the committee member who carried the can for
that had many a change of pants before it hit the jackpot. I think a
lot of the success of *All In The Family* was due to the fact that its
producer Norman Lear was a film man and not a television man if
that makes any sense. Perhaps he didn't understand the rules of
television, or perhaps he was innocent enough to believe that that
was what the American television industry needed – it was certainly what the American television public wanted!

Nevertheless, Hollywood, that modern gold-rush town, with its
attractive Art Deco buildings and its newer, more modern, tall
office blocks reflecting each other in their sun-dimmed windows,
and its name spelled in large white capitals on one of the hills
overlooking it, is the capital city of show business. It attracts the
talented and the untalented alike. It's the place to be if you want
to make it big in show business. Its climate is one of the best
climates anywhere. And its smell, a not unpleasant but quite
peculiar smell, is one of the first things you notice when you
arrive, it assails the senses and gradually clouds almost every
other disposition or combinations of emotional and moral qualities that distinguish an individual; it's the smell of money, freshly
minted money, and as you walk or ride nearer towards Beverly
Hills the smell gets stronger until it becomes almost overwhelm-
ing and paralysing in its potency.

Some never recover from the effect of it, and like most junkies
will do anything for another fix of it. But there are no clinics for it.
There are clinics in abundance for every other drug legal or
illegal, and every other habit-forming substance or neurosis, but
not for this one. Its sufferers have to suffer. Oh, the joy of those
lush hundred-dollar bills! Forget all those high-flown ideals you
arrived with, this is what it's really all about. This is why you
made the trip. You sit out by the pool on a sun lounger, waiters
hovering at your elbow, surrounded by the beautiful people.

Wealth and power is what's beautiful here, not physical or mental refinements. You're in no mood here to sit about wasting time on thinking what might make a good show, all those ideas of art and whatever you arrived with have been supplanted by dreams of avarice. What makes a good show here is what makes the money flow. Carl Reiner, that very able comedy writer and director, told me when I first arrived,

. 'What you'll see here,' he said, 'is a mountain of shit but poke around in it and you'll find diamonds. It's the shit pays for the diamonds.' Never mind about the diamonds you think, how d'you make the shit, 'cos that's where the real money is, that's what they're buying most of.

The fame and wealth to be gained in Hollywood is mythic. Everybody is there to make money, even those who are there to expose it, are there to make money doing it.

Nevertheless, some of the best films ever made were made there and some of the best television, and most of the worst. It's an entertainment factory and a far better factory than the ones I was forced to work in during my youth in Canning Town. And for all the derisive attacks and snide knocking it gets, you have to remember, that most of the great artists in the world have paid it at least one visit in the hope of making some big bucks, and many of the most intensely sensitive of the literati, even the Booker Prize nabobs, dream of Hollywood buying their books. Sam Goldwyn tried to get Bernard Shaw to go to Hollywood. Goldwyn assured Shaw that he would treat his plays with velvet gloves, that their integrity would be preserved at all costs, commercial considerations be damned. A newspaper man called on Shaw to learn the outcome of his conversation with Goldwyn.

'Everything is all right,' Shaw said. 'There is only one difference between Mr Goldwyn and me. Whereas he is after art I am after money.' This is an example of Hollywood madness; it was during the silent days of film, and what kind of job they were going to make of Shaw's plays with the overacting of those silent film stars and the odd caption I must say I find intriguing to imagine. But Sam Goldwyn wasn't finished with Shaw. Sound on film became possible and Hollywood could now make its talkies. Shaw was shown some of these films and asked to reconsider.

'The actors can talk now,' they told him. 'We have sound. Now can we do your plays?'

'No,' Shaw replied. 'The only difference now is the actors speak the captions.'

There are only three things that matter about a show out there: a good rating, a good rating, and a good rating. And it's becoming that way in the UK now. A story told in Hollywood is about two television executives who were walking down a street when they saw a beautiful girl. The first one said, 'Isn't she gorgeous?' and the second one said, 'I don't know yet, the ratings aren't in.'

The ratings are a guide to what the audience is watching and how many of them are watching it, but they're not an accurate guide to what they think about it. They may be watching a show because they've got nothing better to do, or because there's nothing better on, or they're too lazy to get up and turn it off, or turn it over. (As the sales of remote controllers increased so the ratings on a lot of shows decreased.)

Every show must have an audience of some sort, even the most esoteric and erudite, but how large must an audience be before it's viable in television terms? An audience of three million would satisfy the producers of a magazine, or a newspaper, and any dramatic piece that performed in a theatre to that kind of audience would certainly be a long runner, and a source of great pleasure to its author, and the backers for his next work would be queueing up. Or a book! Three million buyers for a book! Not library borrowers. Buyers! How much would that be for the author? Ah, dreams of avarice are never far away.

It has to be something in the nature of the television beast that it must have these mega audiences. Anything under several millions and it's 'Let's look for something else' time. (Ten million is getting very near the bottom line for continued television success in the UK.) *Till Death* . . . was clocking about twenty-six million at the beginning. If it hadn't been for the large audience, and the critical approval, it would probably have been taken off because of the controversial storm it generated. The executive who would have dared to take it off in those days though, would have had to have been either very brave or raving mad, probably both, so very large audiences have other qualities apart from the wealth they can spawn.

Anyway, in Hollywood no one is interested in minority appeal no matter how favoured or precious the minority is. Which is a shame really because it prevents a lot of good work being done.

During one of my first visits to Hollywood I stayed in the Beverly Hills Hotel, aka the Pink Palace. It's one of the oldest hotels there I believe and also one of the best. It was, and still is, a rendezvous for most of the biggest names in show business. It boasts the famous Polo Lounge where the élite meet to eat, and you have to book breakfast reservations, even if you're living in the hotel. It's where Neil Simon set his film *California Suite*.

Anyway, it was one of those wonderful sunny mornings which I like so much about Los Angeles, and I decided to go for a walk. A mistake in that part of the world. I set off, refusing the car the Bell Captain urged me to take. I was new to the scene. It was a glorious day, with blue skies like the song, and I wanted to walk and bask in the sun. *All In The Family* was the top show out there, I was its creator, and I wanted to take a stroll round Beverly Hills, and sort of case the joint.

So I started to walk through the streets of Beverly Hills, the streets the stars lived on, where every house was like a miniature stately home, and some of them not so miniature. The wealthy English aristocracy hide their great mansions in miles of parkland away from prying eyes, but not here: here the attitude is, 'If you got it, flaunt it!' It's a wonder they don't have the price they paid for the house written up outside, or how much it costs them to live in it. It's like, 'Look at me, see my house? I've made it, right? Fuck what anybody says about me or my films, I'm big! I'm laughing all the way to the bank, right?'

And while I was walking, not minding my own business, but peering over the ornate walls and hedges that surrounded these badges of wealth and influence, a police car pulled up, and these two large unfriendly-looking cops got out of it. One of them had a belly that was as big as a pregnancy that was ready to terminate.

He wore dark glasses, and was chewing gum, and had a bloody great gun hanging from his hip. The other one was a bit slimmer, he looked only about four months gone. He also wore dark glasses. Which I was to learn was almost obligatory among LA cops, as was the gum. Who was copying who? Was it life copying art again?

The bigger of the two confronted me, stick side as they call it. The cop has to stand stick side of you so you can't grab his gun, which of course, I had no intention of doing. The thought didn't even cross my mind. While the other one wandered round me, hand on his gun, watching me through his beady dark bins.

'Whadaya doin'?' the bigger one snarled.

'Walking,' I said.

'Whadaya mean, walking?' he asked, belligerent.

'Well,' I said, 'it's what we do in England. You put one foot in front of the other and it propels you along.'

'Oh, a limey,' he said, 'a smart-arse limey are ya? Whadaya doing here?' he asked.

'I'm here on a visit,' I said.

'Where's ya passport?' he asked.

'It's at my hotel,' I told him. At that time, the hotel retained your passport until you checked out. I don't know why. Probably didn't trust UK passport holders, I imagine. Thought we'd run off without paying the bill, I suppose. We were only allowed to take so much money out of the country in those days.

'Which hotel?' the cop said.

'The Beverly Hills,' I told him. With that he began to look more friendly. I might have looked suspicious to him, but the Beverly Hills Hotel was well above reproach and they didn't let rooms to bums. If I was all right by the Beverly Hills Hotel, I was beginning to be all right by him.

'What you in, show biz?' he asked, a lot more amiable now.

'Yeah,' I said.

'Whadaya do?' he asked.

'Well, I'm a writer,' I said.

'Whadaya write?' he asked.

'Well,' I said, 'it's a show you wouldn't know about, it's an

English show called *Till Death Us Do Part*, but over here it's called *All In The Family*.'

'You write Archie Bunker?' he asked.

'I'm the creator,' I said.

'D'you hear that?' he asked his partner. 'This guy here created Archie! Wow! Hey, where you headed for?' he asked.

'I was going to Sunset Boulevard,' I said.

'You in a hurry?' he asked.

'No,' I said.

'Get in the car,' he said. So I got in.

'D'you mind coming down to the precinct? The guys there would love to meet ya.'

'All right,' I said, and to the precinct they took me.

'Hey fellas,' he called, as we entered, 'this is the guy who created Archie Bunker!' And they got me pissed, well pissed. Archie the bigot, like Alf the bigot, was very popular.

Food in America is very plentiful, not for everyone perhaps, but it is if you live in the Beverly Hills Hotel. I ordered a steak and it was so large it covered the plate, and it was a large plate. Back in Canning Town, in the old days, it would have been enough meat for a family of five.

'What cut is this?' I asked the waiter, 'plate size?' He wasn't amused. He was a real waiter. Not one of the many college kids who wait on table these days in LA, who may be your waiter this year and the new Head of Comedy next year. I couldn't eat all of the steak, I hardly made any impression on it at all.

When he came to clear the table, the waiter looked a bit put out at the amount of steak I'd left uneaten, not because of any consideration for the chef's feelings at what might be construed as a slur on his cooking, it was more concern for his tip . . . there's no built-in service charge out there, they have to rely on the good nature of the customer.

'What's wrong with the steak?' he said.

'Nothing,' I said, 'just too much of it.'

That evening when I sat down for dinner, I looked at the menu, I don't know why, I knew I was going to have steak again. I'm a boring eater. Once I like something I'm loyal to it. (It's like Eric Sykes always ordered egg and chips, take him anywhere, to the most lavish gourmet restaurant, and he would order egg and chips. He and Jimmy Edwards were invited to dinner in the baronial hall of some Duke or other, the table was creaking with venison and other exotic ducal fare, but Eric asked for egg and chips. And he got them. And he drank Chateau Latour with them.) Looking at the menu, though, turned out to be a good idea, because one of the steaks was labelled New York cut. This could be what I want, I thought. New York is a big town, they're city dwellers, sophisticated people, they wouldn't want to eat huge cowboy meals like they do out here on the West Coast. So, that's what I ordered ... and when it arrived it was just as large and plate-sized as the one at lunchtime had been.

At lunch the next day my waiter handed me the menu and watched me read it. He seemed to know what I was going to ask for. There was a small anticipatory smile on his face.

'Steak,' I said.

'How would you like it, sir?' he asked.

'Just remove the horns and wipe its arse,' I said.

Another time, in that strange, mad town, I was invited by Universal Studios to do some research on American religion with the view to a possible comedy series. Religion in America is different, like everything in America is different. They have no organised or established church in America. What they have is basically Christian but a lot more market-oriented than ours. Everything in America is market-oriented. Their real faith is capitalism. I'm a socialist, if I'm anything at all, but I have to admit, that capitalism seems to have a better understanding of human nature. Anyway, not everyone believes in Christianity. Many of the early primitives, including the Greeks and the Romans, to whom we appear to owe most of our civilization, believed in the elements, the gods of fire, the sun, and water, and offered up sacrifices to them. As a Brit, I know that my life is more subject to our weather than anything the church preaches. I can understand worship of the sun. I worship it myself. And I understand that people who live in Ethiopia, and other parched areas of the earth, need water more than they need Christianity. I also know that whoever it was invented electricity made a much more important contribution to our welfare than Christianity. I also know which one I could more easily live without. So the American belief in money is not a belief. I can disparage with any real conviction. I mean, after all, what was I doing in LA myself if I wasn't there searching for a way to make some money?

Anyway, here I was on a tour of the religious circuit looking for comedy material to knead into a format for a network series. What a hope! The material was there in abundance, but I knew the will to go, with the kind of series I was likely to come up with, wasn't. This wasn't my idea. The idea had been conceived by someone in Universal. I was being paid to come up with a pilot they could look at. But I was pretty well convinced it was another case of 'be controversial but try not to offend.' It's hard to satirise a subject that is coming at you and doing the work better itself. Of all the many performers who tried to satirise Maggie Thatcher, none of them managed it better than she did it herself. If she had gone to RADA and learned the basics of the acting craft she might still be Prime Minister today. If you can act with honesty and integrity you've got it made, but Maggie lacked the actor's knack of suspending disbelief. Reagan was better at speaking the lines. He played buddy parts for years in films and was very believable. He came across as the kind of guy you might buy a secondhand car from.

I was given a list each day of various Churches and Ministries to visit. There were kind of Country and Western Churches, with lots of singing, hill-billy type music, and frenzied dancing. Why they imagine God would care for this kind of music baffles me. They must think He's as tone deaf as they are. Drive-in Churches ... yes! Just like the drive-in movies. You sit in your car and plug into the service. I don't know if this particular Church did Holy Communion, but if they did, they brought it out to the car. There was a Church that played jazz and did blues hymns which wasn't bad. And there was one Church that was pure Hollywood pzazz. It was lit like a film set, and its Ministers were all from Central Casting. The day I went, there were eight Robert Redford look-alikes performing. They stood spread across the front of the altar

dressed in sober grey Ivy League suits, bronzed and blond with
gleaming white teeth, all very carefully lit. An older Minister, a
rugged Spencer Tracy type, delivered a homespun sermon with
grave artificial sincerity, but very professionally. Maggie could
have learned a lot from him. His sermon finished, a good many
ladies of the congregation queued to kneel before the Robert
Redford look-alikes and kiss their proffered hands. The ladies
appeared to be experiencing a form of ecstasy.

Then I saw a Church advertised in the *Los Angeles Times* as the
Chapel in the Sky. This I had to visit. It was high up in one of the
banqueting suites on the top floor of the Hilton Hotel. We were
seated in comfortable hotel armchairs, with no hard benches to
kneel on as in the Church of England back home. In fact there was
no kneeling to do at all. The God of this particular sect had no
wish to humble his guests. We were given doughnuts and coffee,
something else that might make the Church of England more
worthy of a visit. The ladies serving the coffee were very generous,
and gave me several refills and another doughnut. It could also
have been called the Breakfast Church as well as Chapel in the
Sky.

The sermon wasn't much, it was the normal uninspired banal-
ity, about how Jesus loved the poor and would welcome them to
his home in Heaven after he'd allowed them to first inherit the
earth. I was certain though, that none of this well-heeled bunch
that formed the congregation here today, would welcome the poor
to their homes in Beverly Hills. But they didn't appear to take
offence at their Lord's obvious preference for the poor. When they
began the collection I twigged why they had been so generous
with the coffee and doughnuts. We were given small envelopes,
the size of a dollar bill, but large enough to hold a good few of
them. I could see that this God didn't deal in coppers or loose
change. It was greenbacks only here.

I got talking to the Minister afterwards and I told him how
impressed I was with his Church. To climb this high I said, to the
thirty-fifth floor of the Hilton, was a real effort on the part of him
and his congregation to make contact with the Lord. He's an old
man I said, and obviously hard of hearing by now, so it must

make it a lot easier to hear your prayers ... you being so much nearer to Him up here. I told him I had been trying to get Pan Am to arrange flights to God. At thirty-five thousand feet up, I said, you're even nearer. Let the First Class pray first, I said, because obviously, their prayers would be more important than Club Class or Economy ... His eyes glazed over. I don't know whether he was thinking ... what a nut! Or what a good idea!

The successful Minister out there doesn't have his own parish like here, he has his own show and keeps a careful eye on the ratings.

16 Following Alf to Australia

All In The Family wasn't the only changed-format version of *Till Death Us Do Part* – the Germans had their own too. The cast were out of the Brecht Ensemble and played it for real with the Alf character made up to look like Hitler. The show was very popular and also very controversial, which led to Willy Brandt, the then German Chancellor, decreeing that it should be taken off the air, which in turn led to such an outcry that he was forced to back off and allow it to continue its run. And popular it was, for what reasons I'm not quite sure. In South Africa the film version of *Till Death* was popular for all the wrong reasons and they queued round the block to see it. So perhaps the Germans, who are not known for a sense of humour, otherwise they would have laughed Hitler off the stage as any reasonable people would (as Alf says, 'Supermen? Bloody Goebbels was a cripple for a start!'), missed the satire, and took him into their hearts as they had done before with their adored prototype, Adolf.

I received a letter from the head of the television company responsible for airing the show, informing me of its success and some of the problems they'd had in mounting it. One of these, he claimed, was that Germany has no history of prejudice and as a consequence this element in the show was a bit bewildering to the average Hun. I wrote back and asked him if they'd forgotten

Hitler already ... and if they had managed to erase him from German history it was a neat trick.

Other countries were doing their own versions of *Till Death*, including Holland who had trouble with the bigotry and prejudice of its central character and were trying, ostrich-like, desperately to turn him into an Alf Van Der Nice. (They are filming another version now which they are doing with a lot less inhibition and is looking very good.)

And then Australia wanted their own version of the show. This came as a bit of a surprise as the British version was always shown there and still is one of the most popular shows on Australian television, and why they would want an Australian version to run in competition with it, I couldn't figure. But they were willing to pay money, first-class air fares, and accommodation for all the family. It sounded like a wonderful three months' holiday in the sun. I asked if I could go via America and Hawaii (a more expensive and much more pleasant route) and they didn't demur one bit. At that time Eric Sykes was going out there with Jimmy Edwards in *Big Bad Mouse* and Warren Mitchell was already out there doing Alf in cabaret, plus I love the sun, so I had no hesitation saying yes, and we were on our way.

Warren phoned me while I was in Hawaii, and said, be prepared, you don't realise how popular the show is out here, and there will be a lot of press at Sydney Airport. And he was right. There was. I was asked to stay on the plane till the other passengers had disembarked, and then I was taken to a room full of cameras from all the various TV stations and the national press of the great Australian nation – all fourteen million of them. That was the size of the population of Australia in those days – our audience for the show in Britain was a lot larger than that.

It was like the arrival of Oscar Wilde in New York and I should have worn a green carnation or something. It was my best arrival anywhere. I found a piece of paper in my pocket, and made out to read from it.

'I have a message from your leader,' I said. 'You have all been reprieved and can return home.' It was during the time of the three-day week when Edward Heath was Prime Minister.

I was told by the press that I had been made an honorary member of all the RSL clubs in Sydney – these are the Returned Servicemen's League clubs and are quite impressive with Olympic-size pools, thousands of one-armed bandits, gaming rooms, large cabaret area with first-class stage facilities and lighting, football pitches and tennis courts, and all the profits are ploughed back into the club.

It was at one of these clubs that Warren, after doing a performance of Alf, came back onto the stage, as himself, and lectured the audience. He told them that their appreciation of Alf was ill-founded, that it was satire, and that Alf should be laughed at and not agreed with. Halfway through his lecture he was grabbed by these Australian rednecks – they're known as Ockers, which roughly translated means bigoted chauvinist pigs – and thrown into the swimming pool fully clothed. When he climbed out he was told that they had paid good money to see Alf Garnett, not to be lectured at by a liberal Pom poofter etc.

'We want Alf,' they said, 'not all that crap you been giving us.' They were most likely South African and German immigrants. Not English surely?

After that Warren gave them some of the most awful of Alf's diatribes, searching I suspect for some sign of sensitivity in that audience, some point where they might say, 'No, that's it, that's enough, you've gone too far this time!' But no matter how awful the views and observations of Alf became; the more vile and raucous Warren made him, the more they liked it.

'You may be a fucking old Pom, Alf,' they used to say, 'but you're one of us!' And this was the type of club I'd been made an honorary member of.

No different from the average Golf Club though, I suppose, so it wouldn't be unfamiliar territory. No different from any of the exclusive gentlemen's clubs in London or elsewhere in the world where to feel superior one has to create an inferior. In Golf Clubs all over the world, that's usually the wives and daughters of the chauvinist members, and almost any kind of ethnic minority, except Asian accountants. The reason for this being that most of the more influential members of these Clubs are wealthy businessmen, and they need someone to help them in their battles with the Inland Revenue. As for poorer blacks, their only chance of getting into a Golf Club is on the end of a broom in the locker room. In one famous Golf Club, that shall be nameless out of cowardice (I still play there occasionally) Vic Oliver was refused membership. I worked with Vic on several radio shows and I asked him about it.

'Why wouldn't they let you join?' The son-in-law of the great Winston Churchill! In our class-structured society. It was unbelievable.

'My handicap,' he said. 'It was my Golf Club handicap.'

'What was your handicap?' I asked him.

'I'm a Jew,' he said. What was good enough for the Churchill family wasn't good enough for this particular Golf Club. It's amazing really. During World War Two, most of its members were fighting on the wrong side. I put up a black in that Club one day, I asked the secretary,

'What happened to that picture of Hitler you used to have in the dining room?'

When the Australian press asked me if I would visit one of these RSL Clubs, I thought, what the hell? I like to keep my mind an open thoroughfare allowing all ideas to pass through it so that I can observe and select. The press didn't think I'd get in to any one of these clubs. They said my hair was too long. It reached to my coat collar. (In those days, I was a pathetic slave to fashion, in appearance only though I must add. My hair was long, and my clothes ridiculously trendy.) And 'long-haired gits' (Alf's immortal words) weren't allowed to lower the tone of these particular citadels of repression and bigotry.

The club I selected was the most antediluvian of these establishments, (and it wasn't easy to find one that stood out from the others) where, like all the others, once the sun was over the yard-arm, they lowered the flag to the plaintive strains of a lone bugler, and if you dared to move or breathe during this ceremony you were in danger of grievous bodily harm. I didn't stay long. I introduced myself to the Secretary, and urged on by his baleful scrutiny of my appearance, left immediately. I had no wish to end up in the pool.

When I came out the press were in a fervour to discover what had happened. I told them I had met the Secretary, and having seen the portraits of the founder members in the board room, and noted their prison haircuts, I quite understood the antipathy to long hair. (Not all Australians are descended from criminals though. There were also the screws and their families.) I explained to the press that we had gone through the nit wars in England, the steel comb, the carbolic soap and all the rest of it, to rid ourselves of such pests as fleas, lice and other bugs, and make it safe to wear long hair, and by persistent, regular washing and grooming of it, prevent the reoccurrence of such things, and promised that while in Australia I would resist going native and continue these English habits of cleanliness. I further informed them that the Secretary had thanked me for my consideration and understanding of his position, and told me, as I had suspected, the rule about long hair wasn't so much prejudice but more a matter of hygiene.

In the early hours of the next morning as we left a restaurant, Warren and I saw the papers. I was front-page news. JOHNNY SPEIGHT SAYS AUSTRALIANS DON'T WASH THEM-SELVES ENOUGH. AUSTRALIANS NOT HYGIENIC SAYS JOHNNY SPEIGHT. DON'T WASH ENOUGH, POM-MIE WRITER ACCUSES AUSTRALIANS.

'I'll run you to the airport if you like,' Warren said.

But one of the better characteristics of the Australians is they're quick to rubbish you (their phrase) but they don't mind you rubbishing them back, although they hadn't rubbished me yet, I'd kind of jumped the gun a bit. But they didn't seem to mind. They took it in fun as it was intended.

One of the things I like about the Australians most, and I like a lot of things about them, they're a great people and I like their attitude, is their sense of humour. They can laugh at themselves. It's a bit like British working-class humour, hard, cruel, not malicious, more ironic, a tool against adversity and useful to have when you're being dumped on. Which is not surprising when you remember their ancestors were able to get out there just by stealing a loaf of bread; they didn't have to fork out hundreds of pounds on air tickets.

Like America, Australia is an immigrant nation, and also like America, they seem to have an inferiority complex about their lack of history. Why this is so I really don't understand. The history of all of the older countries is hardly to be admired, and if they had any sense, they'd try and erase it (like the Germans are trying to erase Hitler), and start again.

Australia is a vast place. It's a continent larger than North America, and yet, as a nation, it struck me as being nothing much more than a collection of seaside towns, and most of them not as good as Bournemouth, and not as safe to paddle in if you're the nervous type like me. There's sharks out there swimming around looking for their lunch and they like us like we like fish and chips. If you can imagine Bournemouth with shark nets and shark-warning helicopters flying overhead ... and these hungry monsters watching and waiting for you to take a dip ... most of us would go back to Margate or Southend for our holidays. It's why Australia breeds such fast swimmers. You've got to be fast if you've got bloody sharks chasing you! Their way of life out there breeds great sportsmen anyway. Well, there's not much else to do except knock a ball about.

Driving through the suburbs of Sydney is like driving through most of our own seaside resorts. The architecture is mainly drab Victorian semis, Dunroamin'-type bungalows, and ugly English-style pubs. That's another sport very popular in Australia. If they could field an Olympic drinking team, they'd win gold every time.

When we were filming in the suburbs of Sydney for *In Sickness And In Health*, I said to the producer,

'We didn't have to come all this way for shots like these. We could have shot 'em in Ruislip.' But then, the flight path into Bangkok is like flying over Ruislip into Heathrow. In fact, a lot of the world's suburbs are beginning to look a bit like Ruislip these days.

Other worrying things for the timid were the redback and funnel web spiders. Killers both. They've got an antidote, but as their bite or sting or whatever can kill you in two minutes flat, you need to be very near hospital when you get stung. The Aussies will tell any anxious inquirer,

'Don't worry. Yer spiders no problem. Just be on the watch when you go out to the dunny [the toilet]. Take a big stick with you.'

Paul Hogan told me about the spiders too. When he was a kid he used to catch them in jam jars (probably even then practising to play Crocodile Dundee). He said the local Council paid them a shilling for every one they caught. It was an effort to try and keep them down – whether it was the spiders they were trying to keep down or the kids, I'm not sure. The local Council in Canning Town had a scheme like that once. Not against spiders – against rats. They paid sixpence for every rat tail you brought them. Well, sixpence was a lot of money in those days, and that scheme led the more entrepreneurial to breed rats. It was a sound economy, they bred fast and furiously and grew quickly, so rat farms started to spring up all over the Borough.

Eric Sykes phoned me from Melbourne where he was working. He was worried about the spiders too. And I told him I'd discovered an even worse killer.

'It's got four wheels,' I said, 'and they call it the car.' In Sydney alone it was killing hundreds more each year than any of the sharks, spiders, snakes, crocodiles, or anything else. The Aussies are terrible drivers and driving there was complicated by some rather bizarre traffic rules. In those days, all traffic had right of way to the right. So, halfway into a crossroads, everyone had right of way. And as they drive on the left, any nut could hurtle out of his driveway, or a side turning, straight into fast-moving traffic. They've stopped that now, but you are allowed to overtake on the inside. And they do, sometimes pushing the car they're overtaking into the path of oncoming traffic. Of course, half an hour out of town and you can drive any way you want because you've driven out of the world of other people and are now in what they call the Outback.

That phrase, the Outback, must have been brought there by

early working-class settlers. It was always a euphemism for sitting on the outside toilet.

'Where is he?'

'He's out the back.' The origins of names, and how they came about, is quite interesting I find. I had an uncle who was the Mayor of West Ham, at a time when the Council was building a new estate, and had decided to name every street after a famous poet. Byron Mews, Shelley Close, Wordsworth Street, that sort of thing. I'm sure most of the tenants would have preferred footballers, or film stars, but this was the Council's stab at a bit of culture. But my uncle, who was Mayor, and had the clout, insisted on one of the streets being named after him: O'Sullivan Avenue. Which in years to come will lead some culture buffs to wonder what O'Sullivan wrote, and who he was to be in such celebrated company.

The Outback, where Paul Hogan filmed *Crocodile Dundee*, is the enormous interior of Australia, where very few have set foot except the aboriginals; and where a sheep farm could be the size of Scotland. All that space they have. Nine-tenths of Australia is empty. It needs people, lots of people, to get it going; but if their skin is a deeper brown than gold, they're not welcome. And yet their pigmentation would suit the climate. They wouldn't have to wear blocker, or cover themselves in sun oil. Anyway, nature has no inhibitions about colour, it provides the pigmentation the climate needs. And there's a rumour, a pretty strong scientific one, that nature is changing the pigmentation of all long-term Australians, and that very soon now, their children will be born a deeper brown to suit the climate. And that'll put the cat among the pigeons when they start appearing. I feel sorry for their wives, because they'll be taking most of the early stick until the penny finally drops. Those redneck members of the RSL Clubs, when their black children start to arrive!

Our producer on *In Sickness And In Health* wanted us to film an episode of Alf in the Outback. Blimey, I had to talk him out of that.

'Who wants to see a lot of boring desert?' I said.

'How d'you know it's just desert?' he asked me.

'I've seen a photo of it,' I said. 'Besides, it's not in Alf's nature to do anything as adventurous as that.' It's certainly not in my nature. Hogan's tales of crocodiles were enough to put anyone off venturing into the Outback!

'Watch your legs,' Hogan said. 'He'll go for them first ... 'cos he's a lazy bugger ... he don't like chasing his food ...' They'll bite your leg off and leave you lying there until they feel like eating you. Imagine lying there with your leg off until the bastard works up an appetite. No, I agree with Hogan, the only good crocodile is one that's been made into a golf bag.

I had already met Paul before I went on my first trip to Australia. He and his manager, John Cornell, came to England to make a film and asked me to write a scene for Warren and Paul, as Alf and Hogan. I ended up playing a part in it, and we struck up a good friendship from then on. So, when I arrived in Australia, they got in touch and became my genial hosts and guides in this strange land. Strange land! Not a bit of it – with my nervous disposition, and being a city boy, I had no intention of leaving Sydney. All I ever really see of foreign parts, is a first-class suite in the best hotel if I can get it, the piano lounge, and a seat by the side of the pool.

On all the trips I've made out to Australia, I've never yet seen either a crocodile, a kangaroo, a funnel web spider, redback, or anything else dangerous. Cockroaches, yes. In some of the best hotels in Sydney. Huge buggers, striding across the suite as if they owned it. One of them, I stamped my feet, shouted, made a lot of noise at it, and all it did, was stop, look back at me, and sneer.

I told the girl at reception. I said, 'I've got a big cockroach in my room.' 'That's all right,' she said. 'Keep it out of sight, don't let the house detective see it.'

I went on chat shows out there. On one of them, because of my cockney accent, they suggested putting up cards like subtitles. Anywhere else I probably wouldn't have minded, but in Australia, with their accent – they should criticise mine! Hogan said to me that if I stayed out there, with my accent I could become the Noel Coward of Australia.

Of all the countries I have visited, my fondest memories are of

Australia, and I'd never dissuade anyone from going there. Living among the easy-going Aussies is very pleasant, and I've always felt very much at home there. It's still very British, although not so class-ridden. Apart from the weather, it's an example of what Britain could be if we had fairer government, and of course, freedom of information. Australian television is not the best in the world, but it's quite an eye-opener to be able to watch politicians being paraded on it, lamely protesting their innocence, after being caught with their hand in the till. It makes great television. I suggested a series based on political corruption called *Your Money In Their Hands*.

*   *   *

An interesting note that may serve as an epilogue to this book, and one I include mainly for the benefit of the gentleman who referred to me as an 'illiterate guttersnipe', I have discovered, and I quote, 'The Ancient History of the Distinguished Surname Speight.'

'The most ancient surname of Speight makes an impressive claim to being one of the oldest Anglo-Saxon surnames on record. The history of the name is closely woven into the intricate tapestry of the ancient chronicles of England, and from scrutinised research of such ancient manuscripts as the Domesday Book the family were here well before the Norman Conquest. This notable English family name, Speight, emerged as an influential name in the county of Kent, where they flourished and played an important role in the political development of England. In the sixteenth century they moved to Ireland and held Derry Castle in County Tipperary. The ancient family motto for this distinguished name is *Vi et Virtute*.'

So, there you have it. Illiterate I may be (I don't understand the motto) but guttersnipe? With forebears like that? More like Anglo-Saxon aristocracy fallen on hard times, if you ask me. I bet many of our present-day aristocratic families can't trace their roots that far back without fear of discovering a foreign connection of some sort. Alf Garnett would be proud of that heritage. His creator is of pure unadulterated Anglo-Saxon blood . . . with just a touch of Irish.

Romantic innit? I feel like I was stolen from a rich pram by gypsies.

P.S. A note for Alf: It looks like the Speights were the first Empire loyalists.